# YOGURT

### by
## LORRY & GERRY HAUSMAN

## PERSEA BOOKS
### NEW YORK

# Contents

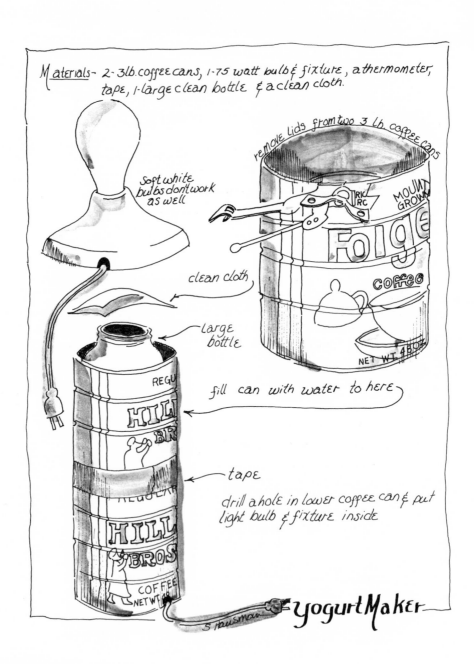

Materials - 2-3lb. coffee cans, 1-75 watt bulb & fixture, a thermometer, tape, 1-large clean bottle & a clean cloth.

remove lids from two 3 lb. coffee cans

Soft white bulbs don't work as well

clean cloth

large bottle

fill can with water to here

tape

drill a hole in lower coffee can & put light bulb & fixture inside

yogurt Maker

S. Hausman

# Yogurt and Me:
# A Momentary History

ONE DAY IN the early 50's my brother and I, in our teens and perpetually hungry for sweets of any kind, discovered in the refrigerator a small container in which was found a substance similar to sour cream, which when stirred became fruity and when tasted was almost sweet enough to deaden the urge for a Hershey Bar. My father was taciturn when it came to things he wished to introduce to us. He said nothing about the small containers which resembled sour cream, except to notice that they disappeared and had to be replaced at regular intervals.

I was by far the less enthusiastic eater. My brother, however, found in yogurt the answer to a major dilemma in his life. He was a varsity wrestler weighing in at 147 pounds. This weight was very hard to keep since he normally weighed about 160. He needed to eat lightly, work out heavily, and look fairly emaciated most of the time.

The discovery of yogurt helped to turn things around. For one thing my brother could eat as much of it as he wanted without gaining weight, and for another it tasted good. And, it was the only snack he could bring to wrestling practice which the other guys wouldn't touch: After the first inquisition—"Hey, look what Hausman's got, an ice cream sundae!"—they left him and his yogurt profoundly alone.

I do not remember that my brother's wrestling proficiency improved or that his teen complexion was purified by yogurt eating, just that he seemed thankful to have found something that tasted good and could be eaten often.

Of course, I ate it too. I liked its slippery consistency on the tongue. And where else could you find whipped prunes or apricots buried under deep layers of snowy cream? For us, yogurt was a great discovery, and if my brother or I had heard Bob Hope's remark on flying over Greenland—"It looked like one big yogurt"—we wouldn't have laughed, we would've gone straight to the refrigerator.

Our father taught us both something else vital about gastronomy: it is not *what* you eat, but *how* you eat it that is important in health and diet. My father ate slowly and thoughtfully. Each morsel was something to be considered before swallowing. He always left his plate clean, bare of any food, except maybe a wishbone. If this sounds exaggerated, I'll let it pass: he was slightly larger than life—as all fathers ought to be, to their children. In his daily life he possessed a sense of ease, a natural grace that said "Go ahead, life is alright for you, wear it with a smile."

So the other day, when I found myself unsmilingly eating fast, I remembered my father, his way of smoothly and pleasurably walking, his unaffected manner of speaking. I could see him cross-legged in his favorite chair, musing over the flavor of a single fig. "Eat your yogurt," he would say, "eat as much as you want, but eat it slowly. It will last longer that way. And so will you."

# Yogurt and the Rest of History: A Cook's Tour

"WELL, OF COURSE, you know there are several basic foods among the Armenians," says William Saroyan, "as well as among the Turks, Kurds, Arabs, Persians, Greeks, Georgians, Roumanians, Bulgarians and two or three other dozen tribes, all the way from the Black Sea to the Siberian Shores of the Pacific: yogurt and pilaf or sour milk and rice."

Saroyan's list might well have included all of Central Asia, from desert sands to frozen steppes; from suburb to city to outpost, yogurt or one of its cousins, such as Kefir or Koumiss, has been eaten or drunk since before the first glories or doubts of recorded time. There was a kind of yogurt referred to in the Old Testament as having been prepared by Abraham (Genesis 18:8) and there also appears to be a reference in Deuteronomy. Persian women creamed away wrinkles with yogurt. Indian legends called it Food of the Gods. Yogurt is mentioned by, among others, Herodotus, Pliny, and Marco Polo. Historical references may be found everywhere there is written history.

Biologically, yogurt is a lactic fermentation which can come from the milk of a cow, goat, buffalo, sheep, horse, camel, reindeer; almost any milk-bearing animal. The discovery of yogurt as an edible food probably was an accident. Sour milk was thrown out, but later retrieved because of its unique power to preserve food immersed in it. Thus something which at first was considered useless was found invaluable for traveling, cooking and storing.

3

Yogurt is variously named *dahi* in India (and was suggested as a staple by Gandhi during the period of his food reforms), *matzoon* or *madzoon* by the Armenians, *joncate* or *junket* by the medieval English, *yalacta* in Norway, *yohurt* or *jugurt* in Turkey, and in the Slavic countries *gjaurt* or *yo-urt.* Yogurt's names are as many as the cultures that use it.

In some of these cultures, yogurt is drunk in a highly acid and alcoholic brew that bubbles and kicks like a mule. In South Russia, it is made from mare's milk and is called kefir. The Cossacks, horse traders and tundra roamers, drank kefir because it was easily carried, helped keep them warm on below-zero nights, and was easily obtained.

Ass's milk is used in India to make a very fine curd of yogurt, more quickly digested by a child than cow's milk. A similar curd is made from camel's milk in the Sahara. Dried yogurt dishes are served in Northern Iraq: two parts yogurt with one part dried par-boiled whole-wheat meal, which is allowed to ferment for a week before an equal amoung of milk is added. The product is fermented, sun-dried and ground into powder. It can be stored for very long periods of time.

A fermented milk product of Scandinavian countries is a drink made from *tette,* a blue meadow flower, the leaves of which are placed at the bottom of a bowl with boiled milk poured over. This mixture, after further processing, has a combined yeast and acid bacteria so strong it can preserve spring milk for use in winter. Its mildness is preferred by those who do not like ordinary yogurt.

How did these natural processes for storing milk become our popular American food, to which we add fresh or stewed fruit, brown sugar or black treacle, molasses or uncooked black currants, salt or pepper, fish, or any other combination of hot, cold, sweet, sour, meaty or noodly edibles? The answer, according to yogurt authority, P. E. Norris, goes back to little Miss Muffet, who as we know was eating her curds and whey (which as we have properly guessed was nothing more than an old timey version of the stuff Dannon has made famous in American supermarkets) when along came a spider— the first press agent in the history of foods—and joined the fun.

4

# Yogurt and Your Health: Fact vs. Fiction

IN A RURAL Indian railway station, Paul Theroux (author of *The Great Railway Bazaar)* overheard a man say he'd been feeling well lately because of his constant consumption of yogurt; he said he drank tons of it because "the bacteria in yogurt keeps down the bacteria in lousy food. Kind of an equalizing thing."

Zaro Agha, a Turk who lived to 162, claimed to have eaten enormous quantities of yogurt all his life. Centenarians from Bulgaria have made similar claims. P. E. Norris in his yogurt book says: "I've heard of yogurt spoken of and seen it written of as a *health food,* whatever that means. In my experience there are no such things as health foods . . ."

A trained nutritionalist from the Federal Trade Commission has testified that yogurt lacks certain well-defined nutrients, so that a person who ate nothing else would be "unable to maintain his nutritional status." Then why do millions of people in Asia who live way below subsistence level use it as a major food source?

Serious studies of yogurt were first made by Elie Metchnikoff, a Russian scientist, co-winner with Paul Ehrlich in 1908 of the Nobel Prize for Physiology and Medicine. Metchnikoff probed the nature of longevity in humans and found we carry in our large intestine a variety of harmful bacteria, which may be a consequence of eating too much animal protein. The bacteria in yogurt are beneficial and helpful, and in a sense, give their lives (they die within 30 seconds to

5

60 minutes after entering the large intestine) to bring about the intestinal equilibrium that Theroux heard about on the railway.

Breast fed babies receive in their mother's milk *bacillus bifidus,* a bacteria which is very similar to the *lactobacillus bulgaricus* of yogurt. In the Near East babies are frequently given yogurt after being weaned at two to three months. Children who refuse to drink sweet milk have something called *lactose intolerance,* which means simply they lack an enzyme that can digest and use milk sugar. Many peoples, especially in the "Third World," have this inability to utilize milk's nutritious properties. For these children and adults, yogurt is not a food but a blessing.

Metchnikoff felt that the burden of human longevity rested entirely on the large intestine and what we put into it. He thought a person who ate yogurt regularly might attain the age of 150.

Long before the appearance of any of Metchnikoff's theories, yogurt had been used as a miracle milk by many ancient cultures who had discovered its curative powers far ahead of western Europe.

Ancient medicinal uses for yogurt range from curing dysentary and all swellings of the stomach, liver and intestine to the purifying of the humours, the cleansing and improvement of the skin, the regulation of the blood, the arousal of the sex drive, and of course, the prolongation of life.

The first major instance of yogurt's use in Europe was when Emperor Francis I, then suffering from steadily declining health which his court physicians were unable to remedy, sent for a Jew from Constantinople, a man famed for miracle cures, and who quickly brought about the complete recovery of the Emperor. His cure was a secret preparation of goat's milk yogurt. Although the method of preparation was left with Francis I, it was safely and securely guarded by his physicians.

The popularity of yogurt today would astonish even Metchnikoff. The short, bearded Russian was certain he could live to at least 100 by consuming fantastic amounts of the stuff. That he died about thirty years before he intended, at 71, ought not to be held against him. What he and his critics overlooked is that yogurt is not, by itself, a miracle milk—it is neither life-giving nor life-saving.

Today we find that there are some cases (especially in the Caucasus) of very old men and women who have eaten yogurt every day of their lives almost since birth. Some are well over 100, but their additional diet consists of other important foods, and yogurt for them is only a small part of an active, healthful life, free from competitive stress.

In our culture, where there's little encouragement for older people to be active members of the society, there's hardly much incentive for a very long life. We tend to want miracles instead of facts. The real yogurt story, if there is one at all, is obscured in advertising and media distortion. What should have the most relevance to the American about yogurt is not "miracle milk," but bacteria.

Apparently, what yogurt does for the intestine is to help move things along so that digestion can take place more gracefully. Certain bacteria—*lactobacillus bulgaricus, streptococcus thermophilus,* and *L. acidophilus*—in yogurt cultures help the digestive process by easing intestinal tension. Sufferers from constipation know the relaxed feeling yogurt can give, and anyone who has experienced an enflamed stomach, due to virus or chronic ailment, and has taken yogurt, knows the soothing effect (after repeated use) its friendly bacteria offer. But only in recent years could the word bacteria be used in a positive context with food. Judging from television ads alone, Americans are more afraid of bacteria entering their homes than the predicted shortage of energy, or the total failure of the economy. Be that as it may, it has been reported an 8 ounce container of yogurt has an antibiotic equivalent to 14 units of penicillin.

The acid medium in yogurt kills *salmonella typhi* in within 30 to 48 hours. Other pathogens are killed by Indian dahi in similar time periods. Doctors are prescribing yogurt to replace the normal intestinal flora which are often wiped out by drug treatments. In addition, it is being used to treat migraine, dysentery, nervous fatigue, ulcers, and acute inflammations of the gums and mouth.

Reporting on the results of a recent yogurt experiment, *The New York Times* stated that the belief that it is good for you may be proven scientifically. In a study which took place in both Africa and Tennessee, involving Masai tribesmen and adult Americans, yogurt was shown to be capable of lowering cholesterol levels in the blood by decreasing the amount the body produces. These findings are expecially interesting in view of the fact that yogurt, like fresh milk, is a relatively high cholesterol food. Dr. Horace Mann, Associate Professor of Bio-chemistry and Medicine at Vanderbilt University, said he believed that the yogurt bacteria produce a substance (probably a small fatty acid) that blocks cholesterol production in the liver.

In this experiment at least Dr. Ilya Metchnikoff's beliefs have found a basis of fact. We are victims, he said, of *autointoxication* from the *wild bacilli* that inhabit our large intestines, and cause hardening of the arteries and premature aging. "A man is as old as his arteries," wrote Metchnikoff.

It is important to remember, however, that the Masai tribesmen (unlike the yogurt faddists of a frozen yogurt shop in New York or San Francisco) purify their veins through exercise as well as diet. The average young Masai walks up to 25 miles a day and even old men cover distances of seven or eight miles. A yogurt-supplemented diet is good for your health, if you exercise on a regular basis, and get proper rest.

# Yogurt and Your Shopping Cart: A Consumer's Guide

IN THE 1930'S you could buy a cup of yogurt, but you had to know where to look. At that time the ethnic connotations of yogurt, and the iron clad, three-meal American diet of plain food were in strict opposition. Even today yogurt manufacturers claim the biggest problem is widespread unfamiliarity with their product. An article in *Esquire* written by Leslie Aldridge Westoff in June, 1973 describes old-fashioned American yogurt: "The family that made it (yogurt) used an array of bottles and jars on the kitchen floor and heated the milk with copper pennies in the pan . . ." The result was a slurpy, oozy, sour-tasting, dripping substance without color or smell.

How did such an eccentric food which few Americans knew how or when to eat become a product readily available in cup, cone, cream, birthday cake, on a stick or in a hamburger bun? Today you can buy yogurt almost anywhere from the Sheraton Boston Hotel to Yogurt Gardens in Beverly Hills, from Wall Street to Wichita. A food as old as civilization is now as ubiquitous as ice cream, a fact which some believe is a major reason for its popularity. They call it "the ice cream without guilt" since you can supposedly eat it without worrying about calories. So let's look at yogurt, not as ancient cure, but as contemporary cultural hero. The rise of yogurt is largely the work of Dannon, the company most of us associate with yogurt making in America. Dannon, originally called Danone, had been making yogurt since 1916 in Barcelona. In 1942 Joe and Juan Metzger came to New York to look up Daniel Carasso, son of the founder of Danone Co. Shortly thereafter, the Metzgers started producing Dannon yogurt in a plant in the Bronx. When Carasso left for Europe after World War Two, the Metzgers stayed on to try and sell yogurt by themselves. It proved a difficult task: as everyone knows, a cultural hero thrives on the exact moment, the necessary appealing ten seconds of historical and psychological time. Yogurt's time had not yet come. Besides its ethnic aura, which was not in vogue right after the war, yogurt had no real place in the American diet. It did not belong on the dinner table and it hadn't the coke and burger personality that would have made it a popular snack. Yogurt just didn't fit in—yet.

The going was rough for the Metzgers, Dannon and yogurt until the great cultural change of the 60's. Then it seemed that everything which had held it back contributed to its success. Some writers claim that the "hippie scene" with its embrace of anything Mom and Dad didn't like may have planted the first seeds of a new yogurt culture. But what really matters is that changes were taking place on every level of American life, and the time had come for a food that was healthful, cheap, ethnic and natural for both body and soul. The idea of yogurt was now acceptable; all that was needed was availability in supermarkets and a little more time.

In 1967 Americans consumed 25 million dollars worth of yogurt. In 1975 they ate nearly 300 million dollars worth—about 200,000 tons of it. Since then the figure has grown even more. As for availability, you can go to any large supermarket and buy over 40 different kinds of yogurt in three or more sizes. Such marketing success cannot entirely be the result of timing. The need for a product must coincide with the product's image and substance. The missing link for commercial yogurt was found by Dannon; the innovation of fruit preserves. When stirred up from the bottom of the container, they made the yogurt less tart, more sweet, thus making it more logical as an ice cream substitute.

Dannon made the discovery of "Sundae Style" back in 1946, and in the late 60's other companies, such as Borden and Sealtest, introduced "Swiss-style" yogurts: those with premixed fruit, preserves or flavorings evenly distributed throughout. Swiss-style is, for many yogurt devotees, tasteless because homogenization has taken away the yogurty tang. One writer described this new flavor as "cloying sweetness." In general, Swiss-style yogurt is for people who don't really like yogurt. And their reasoning is not that they're eating a health food so they can live past 100, but that yogurt simply tastes good.

With Swiss-style yogurts you don't have to stir the fruit up, and in return for this saving of labor, you are rewarded with an ample sprinkling of hearty additives. Even though the label of a particular brand of Swiss-style yogurt may state "All Natural," there is no brand made today without additives. Even when there are no artificial ingredients listed, there will be such "natural" additives as starch, pectin, gelatin and caramel color because taste and texture are more in demand than that good, old fashioned flavor. In the words of one yogurt company President: ". . . If the good Lord made chemicals about the same time he made vegetables and strawberries, aren't they more or less natural, too?"

The best advice I can give is to read the label carefully and know what you are putting in your mouth. Unfortunately, the bacteria in yogurt is really what is good for you, and today there is no federal standard for bacteria count. This means that some manufacturers will make a product that is called yogurt, but which biologically bears little resemblance to the true meaning of the word.

One of the most recent controversies of this kind is over frozen yogurt, enormous quantities of which are being devoured on both coasts. According to *The New York Times,* frozen yogurt may be "The world's first bonafide junk health food because of chemical additives used as stabilizers, emulsifiers, flavorings and colorings." Only Dannon's "Danny-Yo" is 100% natural as advertized. But when you freeze bacteria they die and then, besides the obvious pleasure of eating it, what good is the yogurt for you?

# Yogurt and Your Home: Making Yogurt on Your Own

I REMEMBER THE first time I saw home-made yogurt sitting in a large white porcelain bowl in the bright afternoon sunlight of northern New Mexico. We were at the house of poet David Kherdian, whose mother, Veron, a year later showed us how to make Armenian style yogurt in her home in Fresno, California. Somehow, the white clear light of Santa Fe with snow on the mountains and the dull gold of adobe is part of the flavor of yogurt when I eat it today. But no less so, thanks to Veron, is the vision of hummingbirds darting around the loquat and quince trees, William Saroyan's cousin, Archie, banging his fist on the table and bursting into laughter, and the soft sweet sound of morning doves amidst the lawn sprinklers in hot, hot Fresno.

Yogurt with its absence of color is bound to have visual associations from the places where it was prepared and eaten. The other day I heard a friend speak of making goat's milk yogurt, and how instead of placing the cultured milk in the oven to allow it to thicken, she left it in the warm noon sun on her patio. I could see it there on a thick pine-slab table with baby goats and nannies gently blatting and butting heads. And, if you will pardon my insistence (that is the way it is)—A home is the proper birthplace for a bowl of fresh yogurt.

Aside from the economics (you can save as much as 70% of the cost), many people feel homemade yogurt tastes better than any other kind. Perhaps this is because it's alive. A yogurt culture is not like a cold-cut taken out of the refrigerator and thrown between a couple

12

slices of bread. Yogurt is as alive as you are. Breadmakers say the same thing about working with bread dough. A friend who has a bread and pastry shop told me she believes her loaves vary in quality from day to day, based on her own tactile relationship with the dough. How good her bread is will depend on how sensitive she is to its needs before she places it in the oven to bake.

When Lorry makes yogurt in our home she starts off with very clean utensils and a large glass mixing bowl. (She thinks metal bowls, except stainless steel, will give an unpleasant taste.) She takes a one-quart measuring cup of pasteurized whole milk and adds a half pint of heavy cream to the milk, and places it in a heavy saucepan on the gas burner. Once brought to a boil, the heat is lowered and the milk and cream is simmered for ten minutes. They are then taken off the heat and cooled at room temperature until cool enough to stick a finger in without getting burned—anywhere between 80 and 115 degrees, if you are using a thermometer.

At this point, she adds about a quarter of a cup of plain unsweetened yogurt (either Dannon or Colombo), stirs it thoroughly, places a plate over the top, wraps the bowl in a towel, and puts it in the oven without turning it on. The important thing here is to keep the yogurt in a warm place. An electric oven, because it has no pilot, may not keep it warm enough. If you have a woodstove, you can place the yogurt near or below the stove pipe. If you set it too close to the stove itself, you risk killing the bacteria. Another thing to keep in mind is not to jiggle the yogurt—avoid extremes of movement and temperature.

In four or five hours, Lorry removes the bowl from the oven, puts it in the refrigerator and chills it for two to three hours. This method makes a very creamy, sweet tasting yogurt with which we have pleased both the fussiest devotees and the most suspicious, publicly sworn non-eaters. If you like yogurt that tastes more tart, then let it incubate longer in your oven.

Don't be discouraged if, the first time you try to make your own yogurt, it doesn't come out the way you wanted. Making yogurt is a highly individual matter. It takes a few tries to find your own way.

A quick and easy way to make yogurt is with a thermos bottle. This way you avoid the indecision of where to incubate it. First buy an eight-ounce can of evaporated milk, a container of powdered milk and some plain Dannon yogurt. Mix the evaporated milk with the same amount of hot water and a cup of powdered milk. Bring the liquid to 110 to 120 degrees (no higher), and add four tablespoons of Dannon. Place the mixture in a wide mouth, one quart thermos for six to eight hours. Afterward, cool in refrigerator.

Lorry also likes to make yogurt with a Salton Yogurt Maker. One quart of whole milk is mixed with one third cup of powdered milk, then brought to a boil and cooled. The Salton method includes a very handy spoon thermometer that tells you when to add the heaping tablespoon of plain yogurt. Stir it well, pour it into the clean cups and plug in the yogurt maker. Five to ten hours later, depending on how tart you like it, you have a nice creamy yogurt. You should experiment with the Salton to achieve your own favorite texture and taste. [You may want to look into other brands of yogurt makers such as Balkan, Yogomatic and Yogutera, which also have good reputations.]

Here is another variation of home yogurt making. Get yourself a water thermometer, a clean half-gallon container with a tight-fitting lid, one half gallon reconstituted powdered milk with one to one and a half times as much powder as is normally used, three tablespoons of Dannon plain yogurt for starter. Place the thermometer in a pot of water that is big enough to hold the yogurt jar, and be ready to put it near your heat source—try a heating pad for this purpose. Mix the yogurt with the milk, cover, place in the pot, fill to the brim of the jar with water, and leave sitting for eight to ten hours. If the yogurt is watery and tastes more like milk than yogurt, give it a few more hours. If the culture is sour, try a lower temperature or a shorter time with the next batch.

One way to entirely eliminate milk from yogurt making—for flavor, health, allergenic or whatever reasons you wish—is by using soymilk. In Japan soymilk is considered a natural medicine for diabetes, heart disease, high blood pressure, hardening of the arteries, anemia and digestive disorders. Due to its high nutritive value, low calorie and cholesterol content (it has 51% more protein than dairy milk, 12% fewer calories, 24% less fat), soymilk is an excellent milk substitute for freshly weaned infants, growing children, and adults. You can make fresh soymilk from the powdered sold in natural food stores. Allow the soymilk to cool to slightly warmer than body temperature (105 to 110 degrees). Remove thin film from surface of soymilk and stir one teaspoon commercial yogurt into soymilk, mix and pour into a clean jar. Cover and allow to stand at room temperature (70° F. or above) for 14 to 18 hours. To decrease fermentation time, you can either add a teaspoon of honey before mixing the yogurt and soymilk together, or add a little more starter, or use an incubator set at 100 to 110 degrees.

14

Here is yet another idea for non-dairy yogurt made from almond milk. Almonds are high in vitamins, minerals, and essential amino acids. The additional ingredients in the following recipe combined with almonds make an extraordinarily healthful and delicious food.

To make five quarts of almond milk, blend together the following: one gallon of organic apple juice; approximately two to two and one half pounds (about four to five cups) of almonds, either finely ground or in the form of nut butter; one half pound (seven to eight tablespoons) of finely ground sesame seeds or four to five tablespoons of sesame tahini; one tablespoon of Brazil nuts, finely ground or in the form of butter (optional); one tablespoon of powdered cinnamon; one tablespoon of powdered nutmeg; one tablespoon of vanilla; one tablespoon of lecithin (optional).

Get a package of yogurt or kefir starter, sterilize a quart bottle, heat some unstrained almond milk to 180° (too hot to touch but not boiling), then when the milk has cooled to room temperature, pour it into the sterile container and add the yogurt or kefir starter. Store the liquid at room temperature for 24 hours. To make more yogurt, repeat the above procedure using three tablespoons of almond milk in place of the starter.

Although Lorry and I enjoy using our automatic Yogurt Maker, you may want to build your own yogurt maker, and have complete control over the entire process. You can easily make an incubator with a couple of coffee cans, an electric cord, a 75 watt bulb and a thermometer.

Punch a hole in the bottom of one of the cans, and place your light socket inside with one light cord going through the hole on the outside. The second can sits on top of this one with the bottom facing down (it will later be filled to half full with water). The 75 watt bulb should keep the temperature at about 110° to 120°, but to be sure, check this with the thermometer.

Find a clean glass or jar to go inside the top coffee can, and fill it with warm milk. Mix in two to four tablespoons of yogurt (the more you use, the faster the batch will congeal) and allow it to sit for at least four hours immersed in the warm water. Make sure top of jar is covered with a clean cloth.

After four hours, check the yogurt to see if it has the taste and texture to your liking. If it hasn't congealed yet, incubate longer or experiment with a bulb of higher wattage.

Although we usually add flavorings after we make plain yogurt, you can make flavored yogurts right in your yogurt maker. Here are some simple recipes for flavored yogurts.

15

# CARROT YOGURT

⅓ c. powdered milk
3  c. milk
¼ c. plain yogurt
4  large carrots

Combine the carrots, peeled and cut in small pieces, the powdered milk and 2 cups of milk. Blend until everything is smooth. Add milk until you have four cups. Bring to a boil, remove from heat, then cool to 115° F. Stir in culture, pour in containers and keep warm for 5 hours. Chill well before eating.

# COFFEE YOGURT

Add ½ cup strong coffee and 2 tbsp. sugar to regular yogurt recipe.

# CUCUMBER YOGURT

1  lb. cucumbers
3½ c. milk
¼  c. plain yogurt

Peel cucumbers, grate and squeeze liquid out through cheesecloth. Heat milk to a boil, remove from heat and cool to 115° F. Add culture and cucumbers. Stir well and pour into containers. Cover and keep warm for 5 hours. Chill before eating.

# *Yogurt Dips and Spreads*

## AVOCADO DIP

1   soft ripe avocado
1   c. yogurt
¼ c. mayonnaise
½ tsp. salt
½ tsp. seasoning salt
½ c. parsley, finely chopped
¼ c. scallions, finely chopped

Mash avocado well; add yogurt and mayonnaise. Mix well. Add salt and seasoning salt. Fold in chopped parsley and scallions. Serve with chips.

## ANCHOVY SPREAD

1   small pkg. cream cheese
1   can flat anchovies, cut
½ medium Bermuda onion, grated
½ c. yogurt
Dash of Worcestershire Sauce

Mix all ingredients well. Use as spread for crackers. If you want a thinner consistency, add a little more yogurt.

# GREEN CHILI DIP

1  8-oz. pkg. cream cheese
½ c. yogurt
½ c. mayonnaise
5  tbsp. chopped green chili
4  tbsp. minced onion
Dash of salt

Mix all ingredients in order given. Chill overnight. Serve with tortilla chips.

# CITRUS DIP

1  c. plain yogurt
1  tbsp. frozen orange juice concentrate
1  tsp. lemon juice
4  tsp. sugar

Mix all ingredients together. Place in small bowl in center of fruit.

# CLAM DIP

2  c. yogurt
1  can minced clams, drained
½ pkg. cream of leek soup mix
Dash of Worcestershire Sauce

Combine all ingredients and let stand for 30 minutes.

# CURRY-CHUTNEY DIP

1  8-oz. pkg. cream cheese
1  tbsp. curry powder
½ tsp. garlic powder
½ c. chopped chutney
½ c. yogurt
2  tbsp. milk

Blend cheese with curry and garlic powder. Add chutney, yogurt and milk. Serve with pieces of raw vegetables.

## CUCUMBER AND MINT

3  cucumbers
4  c. thin yogurt
½  tsp. salt
1  clove garlic, pressed
1  tbsp. dried mint

Peel and slice cucumbers in thin slices. Blend yogurt, salt, garlic and mint together. Add cucumbers and chill. Serves 4.

## CHEESE MOUSSE

2  tsp. unflavored gelatin
¼  c. cold water
2  c. yogurt
2  tsp. Italian salad dressing mix
¼  c. crumbled bleu cheese
1  c. cottage cheese (country style)

Soften gelatin in cold water. Place over boiling water and stir until gelatin dissolves. Stir into yogurt. Add salad dressing mix, bleu cheese and cottage cheese. Beat until well blended. Pour into small loaf pan and chill until firm. Unmold. Spread on crackers.

## DRAINED YOGURT

You can replace cream cheese with drained yogurt. All you do is spoon 1 qt. of plain whole-milk yogurt into 3 layers of cheesecloth. Then tie the yogurt into a bag and hang from the rack on your refrigerator with a bowl underneath to catch the liquid. Leave overnight and the next morning you will have a little over a cup of creamy yogurt cream cheese. Mix it with salt, pepper, scallions or chives. Spread it on crackers or bread, or use it in recipes calling for thick yogurt or cream cheese.

# HOT MUSHROOM DIP

1    lb. fresh mushrooms
1    clove garlic, crushed
1    small onion, grated
2    tbsp. butter
⅛    tsp. mustard
½    tsp. soy sauce
⅛    tsp. paprika
⅛    tsp. salt
⅛    tsp. pepper
1    tbsp. flour
1    c. yogurt

Brown mushrooms, garlic and onion in butter. Combine mustard, soy sauce, paprika, salt, pepper and flour with a little yogurt to make a paste. Add to the mushrooms. Blend in remaining yogurt and stir over low heat until thick. Do not boil. Serve with chips. 2 cups.

# YOGURT VEGETABLE DIP

½    c. cottage cheese
1    tbsp. finely grated carrot
2    tsp. finely grated onion
1    tsp. finely grated green pepper
½    tsp. salt
⅛    tsp. garlic salt
Dash of white pepper
1    c. (8 oz.) all-natural lowfat yogurt, plain

In a small mixing bowl beat cottage cheese, blend in carrot, onion, green pepper, salt, garlic salt and pepper. Beat until fairly smooth. Fold in yogurt. Cover and chill. Use as a dip for chips or raw vegetables.

# *Yogurt Soups*

## YOGURT CREAM SQUASH SOUP

1   lb. sliced zucchini
½   c. water
1   tbsp. minced onion
¼   tsp. pepper
½   tsp. salt
½   tsp. parsley flakes
3   tsp. chicken stock
2   tbsp. butter
2   tbsp. flour
⅛   tsp. white pepper
¼   tsp. ground celery seed
1   c. milk
½   c. light cream
Yogurt
Paprika

Combine first 5 ingredients and 1 tsp. chicken stock. Cook zucchini until tender and water is almost gone. Put through a sieve. Melt butter in saucepan; add flour, remaining stock and seasonings. Blend well. Add milk and cream; simmer, stirring until thickened. Stir in zucchini. Add milk if too thick. Top with yogurt and sprinkle with paprika. Serves 5.

# YOGURT PUMPKIN SOUP

4   c. shredded green pumpkin
2   tbsp. butter
4   tbsp. flour
4   c. water
1   bay leaf
salt and pepper to taste
½   c. evaporated milk
½   c. yogurt

Use only a pumpkin that has no yellow. Peel, remove seeds and shred with cheese grater. Set aside. Brown butter and flour in a large frying pan; add water slowly. Cook with bay leaf, salt and pepper for a few minutes. Add pumpkin and cook for 20 minutes. Remove from heat and add evaporated milk mixed with yogurt. Stir and serve. Serves 6.

# YOGURT BEET BORSCH

6   large beets
water
3   tbsp. lemon juice
¼   c. sugar
1   tsp. salt
2   egg yolks
1   c. yogurt

Peel and grate beets. Cook in 3 pints water until tender. Add lemon juice, sugar and salt, simmer for 5 to 15 minutes longer. Beat egg yolks with 1 tbsp. cold water; gradually add hot beet mixture, stirring constantly. Chill. Beat yogurt into mixture before serving. 6 servings.

# YOGURT BEEF BORSCH

1    small head cabbage
3    med. potatoes
3    qt. beef stock
2    Spanish onions
1    28-oz. can tomatoes
1    bunch carrots
1    tbsp. chopped dill
⅓    lb. butter
1    c. yogurt

Peel potatoes and carrots. Halve one potato and slice the rest of the potatoes and carrots very finely. Boil the carrots and potatoes in 3 qts. salted water. Slice onions and saute in butter until brown. Add finely shredded cabbage and fry, stirring frequently. Add tomatoes and dill. Simmer for a few minutes. When carrots and potatoes are done, mash the halved potato with yogurt and return it to the pot. Add contents of the frying pan and simmer for 45 minutes. Serves 6.

# BEEF BORSCH

1    bunch beets
1    c. tomatoes
4    c. water
1    lemon, chopped
½    lb. stew beef, cut in 1-inch cubes
1    tbsp. lemon juice
1    tbsp. sugar
¼    tsp. salt
4    eggs
Yogurt

Combine beets, tomatoes and water; simmer with onion and meat for 30 minutes. Add lemon juice, sugar and salt. Boil another 30 minutes. Beat eggs with a little salt and add slowly to hot borsch. Garnish with yogurt. 6 servings.

# GREEN BEAN-YOGURT SOUP

¾  lb. snapped green beans
1   qt. thin yogurt
½  tsp. pepper
1   tbsp. flour

Cook beans in salted water until tender. Add yogurt, heat thoroughly. Add pepper. Make a paste of flour dissolved in small amount of milk, stir in and heat to a boil, remove from heat and let cool. Chill and serve. Serves 6.

# BARLEY YOGURT SOUP

1   c. barley
2   c. water
4   c. creamy yogurt
5   c. chicken bouillon
2   eggs, beaten
2   tsp. salt
⅓  c. butter, melted
2   tbsp. mint, crushed
1   tsp. honey

Soak barley overnight in 2 c. of water. Drain. Beat the yogurt and eggs together and blend into the barley and the bouillon. Add ¼ c. melted butter, mint and honey. Serve hot or cold. 5 servings.

# HONEYMOON WHEAT GERM SOUP

1   (8 oz.) carton plain yogurt
2   tbsp. chopped green onion
½  c. chopped celery
¼  c. parsley sprigs
3   tbsp. wheat germ with sugar and honey
¼  tsp. basil leaves, crushed
1   tsp. sugar, optional
Several grinds black pepper
Grated parmesan cheese

Combine all ingredients except cheese in electric blender. Whir until chunky-smooth. Chill thoroughly. Serve with grated cheese and additional chopped green onion on top, if desired. Makes 2 servings.

## AVOCADO FRUIT SOUP

1   can (30 oz.) fruit cocktail
1   c. water
2   beef bouillon cubes
1   tsp. salt
1   clove garlic, minced
Juice and grated rind of 1 lemon
3   ripe avocados, peeled, pitted and quartered
½   cup sour cream
½   c. plain yogurt
¼   c. white wine
2   ripe tomatoes, chopped

Drain fruit cocktail, saving syrup. In saucepan mix together saved syrup, water, bouillon cubes, salt, garlic, lemon juice and lemon rind. Bring syrup mixture to simmer, stirring occasionally until bouillon cubes are dissolved. Remove from heat. In blender whir avocados, sour cream, yogurt and wine until smooth; pour into large bowl and stir in syrup mixture thoroughly. Add fruit cocktail and tomatoes. Chill thoroughly. Takes at least 2 hours. Serves 6.

## SUMMERTIME SOUP

For hot summer days, simply mix two cups of plain yogurt with one can of condensed tomato soup. Season this lightly with celery salt and onion salt, sprinkle with fresh chopped olives and parsley.

# Yogurt Main Course Dishes: Beef, Pork, Veal, Lamb

## BEEF SUPREME

1   clove garlic
½   c. chopped onion
2   tbsp. oil
1   lb. sirloin, cut in 2-inch strips
½   tsp. salt
⅛   tsp. pepper
¼   c. flour
1   3-oz. can sliced mushrooms
2   tbsp. catsup
½   to 1 c. beef bouillon
½   c. yogurt
Cooked egg noodles
Poppy seed

Saute garlic and onion in oil. Dredge beef in seasoned flour; add to onions. Add mushrooms, catsup and ½ c. bouillon. Cover and simmer for 30 minutes, adding more bouillon as needed. Add yogurt, simmer for 30 minutes. Alternate layers of beef mixture with noodles in casserole. Cover and refrigerate overnight; sprinkle with poppy seed. Bake at 325° F. for 30 minutes. If necessary add more bouillon during baking. 6 servings.

# BEEF RHAPSODY

2   lbs. boneless beef, cut in 1 inch cubes
¼   c. flour
1½  tsp. salt
¼   tsp. pepper
3   tbsp. cooking fat
1   c. water
3   tbsp. grated onion
1   bay leaf
1   pkg. (10 oz.) frozen peas
1   c. yogurt
1   tbsp. prepared horseradish

Combine flour, salt and pepper. Dredge meat in seasoned flour. Brown in fat or drippings. Pour off drippings. Add water, onion and bay leaf. Cover tightly and cook slowly 2 hours. Add frozen peas and continue cooking 20 to 30 minutes or until meat is tender and peas are done. Discard bay leaf. Add yogurt and horseradish and heat through. 6 servings.

# BALKAN BEEF

2   lbs. boneless beef for stew, cut in 1-inch cubes
1   can (4½ oz.) sliced mushrooms
Water
1   beef bouillon cube
½   tsp. dill seed
¼   c. flour
1   tsp. salt
¼   tsp. pepper
3   tbsp. lard or drippings
1   can (8 oz.) tomato sauce
1   medium-sized onion, quartered
2   c. diagonally-cut celery
½   pint plain yogurt
4   oz. noodles, cooked

Drain and reserve mushrooms. Add water to mushroom liquid to equal ¾ cup, heat to boiling, add bouillon cube and stir to dissolve. Add dill seed to liquid and set aside. Combine flour, salt and pepper.

Dredge beef cubes in seasoned flour. Reserve remaining flour. Lightly brown beef in lard or drippings. Pour off drippings. Add mushroom-dill liquid, tomato sauce and onion and stir to combine. Cover and cook over low heat for 1 hour. Add celery, cover and cook 1 hour longer, or until meat is tender. Stir in reserved flour and mushrooms. Stir a small amount of hot sauce into yogurt, then stir into meat and remaining gravy. Place uncovered over low heat until sauce is warm. Serve over noodles. 6 to 8 servings.

## MUSHROOM YOGURT STEAK

| | |
|---|---|
| 1 | round steak |
| 1 | clove garlic |
| ¼ | c. flour |
| 2 | tbsp. paprika |
| 1 | tsp. pepper |
| ¼ | c. shortening |
| ¼ | c. sliced onion |
| 1 | 3-oz. can mushrooms, drained |
| ½ | c. yogurt |

Cut steak into four pieces and rub each piece well with cut garlic clove. Combine flour, paprika, salt and pepper. Pound into steak. Brown meat in hot shortening. Put onions and mushrooms on top. Cover and cook over low heat for 2 hours. Add liquid if needed. Remove steak. Spoon excess fat from liquid in pan; add yogurt. If too thick, dilute with water or bouillon. Heat and serve sauce over meat.

## RED WINE AND BEEF IN YOGURT SAUCE

| | |
|---|---|
| 2 | lb. beef round, tenderized |
| 1 | 10-oz. pkg. thin noodles |
| 1 | garlic clove |
| 3 | onions, sliced thin |
| 4 | tbsp. butter |
| 2 | cans beef gravy |
| 1 | c. yogurt |
| salt and pepper to taste | |
| ½ | c. Burgundy wine |

Cut beef into 1-inch cubes. Cook noodles. Saute garlic and onions in butter until onions are transparent. Remove onions. Brown beef cubes in pan drippings; add gravy, yogurt, salt, pepper and onions. Put noodles in casserole dish. Pour meat mixture over noodles. Bake in 325⁰ F oven for 1½ hours or until meat is tender. Add wine and bake 15 minutes longer. 6 servings.

# WILD RICE STROGANOFF

| 2 | lb. beef round, tenderloin or sirloin |
| 4 | to 8 tbsp. butter, melted |
| 1 | c. onion, chopped |
| 1 | clove garlic, minced |
| ½ | lb. fresh mushrooms, chopped |
| 2 | to 3 tbsp. flour |
| 2 | tsp. dry mustard |
| 2 | tbsp. catsup |
| ½ | tsp. salt |
| ⅛ | tsp. pepper |
| 1 | can beef bouillon |
| ½ | c. dry white wine |
| 1½ | c. yogurt |
| 4 | c. cooked white rice |
| ½ | c. cooked wild rice |
| | Fresh parsley |

Cut beef in strips; brown in 1 tbsp. butter in skillet. Remove beef and add remaining butter to pan. Saute onion, garlic and mushrooms about 5 minutes. Remove from heat; stir in flour, dry mustard, catsup, salt and pepper. Gradually add bouillon; bring to a boil, stirring constantly. Reduce heat and simmer 5 minutes. Blend in wine and yogurt. Add beef; simmer until hot. Toss rice together. Surround stroganoff with rice; sprinkle with parsley. 6 servings.

# SPICY YOGURT BEEF KABOBS

2 lbs. boneless beef chuck, cut in 1½-inch chunks
1½ c. plain yogurt
¾ c. chopped onion
1 tsp. minced garlic
1 small dried hot chili pepper, chopped (optional)
¾ tsp. ground cumin seed
½ tsp. nutmeg
¼ tsp. salt
¼ tsp. cinnamon

Toss beef chunks with all remaining ingredients. Cover and refrigerate overnight. String beef on skewers. Barbecue over hot coals about 15 minutes, turning every 5 minutes. Makes 4 to 6 servings.

# MEATBALLS IN YOGURT

1 lb. hamburger
½ c. bread crumbs
¼ c. chopped onions
½ c. whole milk
1 tsp. salt
⅛ tsp. pepper
3 tbsp. butter

Combine ingredients except butter and shape into balls. Brown in butter. Remove from pan and keep warm. Pour most of the grease from the pan.

### SAUCE
¼ c. butter
¼ c. flour
2¼ c. thin yogurt
¼ tsp. salt
2 tbsp. sugar
1½ tsp. dry mustard
1 egg, beaten
⅛ tsp. pepper

Combine ingredients to make gravy. When thick, add meatballs and simmer until ready to serve. Serves 4.

# BEEF 'N WHEAT GERM IN POCKET BREAD

4   pocket bread rounds, halved
½   lb. lean ground beef
1   medium onion, coarsely chopped
2   large cloves garlic, minced
2   tbsp. cooking oil
¾   c. vacuum packed wheat germ (regular)
2   (8 oz.) cartons plain yogurt
1½  tsp. dried mint leaves, crushed
1   tsp. oregano leaves, crushed
½   c. chopped celery
½   c. minced parsley
¾   tsp. salt
    Chopped tomatoes, shredded romaine lettuce and thinly sliced cu-
    cumbers

Wrap bread in foil. Place in 350° oven 15 minutes or until heated through. Meanwhile saute beef, onion and garlic in oil until browned. Stir in wheat germ, 1½ c. yogurt, mint leaves, oregano, celery, parsley and salt. Cook over low heat a few minutes, stirring gently until heated through. Spoon into pocket bread. When serving, pass around tomatoes, lettuce, cucumbers and remaining yogurt to add to pockets as desired. Makes 4 servings.

# YOGURT BURGER

1   lb. ground beef
1   c. chopped onions
1   egg, beaten
1   c. yogurt
¾   tsp. salt
¼   tsp. pepper
1   recipe buttermilk biscuits
1   c. grated cheese

Grease a 9-inch square baking dish. Fry ground beef until done. Remove beef and cook onions until transparent. Combine egg, yogurt, salt and pepper; add ground beef. Divide biscuit dough in half. Roll out each part to fit the baking dish. Put 1 half in the bottom of the dish. Top with beef mixture, onions and cheese. Fit other half on top. Bake for 30 minutes in 400° F oven. 4 servings.

# GARLIC / YOGURT BURGERS

1    lb. ground round steak
1    tsp. salt
⅛   tsp. pepper
2    cloves garlic, pressed
1    onion, minced
1    c. yogurt
1    c. bread crumbs

Mix ground round, salt, pepper, onion, garlic and add yogurt slowly. Put the bread crumbs in, mix and then shape patties and broil until brown on both sides. Serves 6.

# CURRIED BEEF AND RICE

1½  lbs. lean ground beef
2    c. sliced onions
1    c. uncooked rice
2½  c. beef broth (made from bouillon cubes)
2    tsp. salt
1    can (4 oz.) sliced mushrooms, drained
1    tsp. curry powder
1    tbsp. Worcestershire sauce
1    carton (8 oz.) yogurt (1 c.)

Cook beef and onions in lightly greased skillet until meat is no longer pink. Stir frequently to crumble meat. Add rice and continue cooking until meat has browned. Add broth, salt, mushrooms, curry powder, and Worcestershire sauce. Heat to boiling. Stir well, reduce heat, cover, and simmer 20 minutes. Serve hot, topped with dollops of yogurt. Sprinkle with chopped parsley, if desired. Makes 8 servings.

# LASAGNE

½   lb. ground beef
½   lb. sausage
½   c. onion, chopped
1    6-oz. can tomato paste
2    8-oz. cans tomato sauce

½  lb. fresh mushrooms, sliced
1  garlic clove, pressed
1  tsp. basil
1  tsp. parsley
1  tsp. salt
½  tsp. oregano
¼  tsp. pepper
1  qt. whole-milk yogurt, drained
½  c. Parmesan cheese
1  c. walnuts, chopped
¾  lb. mozzarella cheese, shredded
½  lb. lasagne noodles

Brown the beef and sausage and pour off the fat. Saute onion, garlic and mushrooms. Combine the tomato paste, sauce, mushrooms, onion, garlic, basil, parsley, salt, oregano, walnuts and pepper. Simmer ½ hour on low heat. Cook and drain lasagne noodles. Put ⅓ of the meat sauce in 12 x 8 x 2 baking dish. Add layer of drained noodles, layer of drained yogurt, mozzarella cheese and 2 tbsp. of Parmesan. Add the second third of the meat sauce and then ingredients in the same order ending with last meat sauce and a sprinkling of Parmesan. Bake at 350° F for 30 minutes or until hot and bubbly.

## LEEK LASAGNE

6  tbsp. olive oil
4  c. finely sliced leeks
1½ tbsp. salt
½  tsp. pepper
1  tsp. hot red pepper
1  onion, minced
1  lb. ground round steak
1½ c. tomato sauce
1  tbsp. dried mint
½  lb. lasagne noodles, cooked and drained
1½ to 2 c. drained yogurt
3  cloves garlic, finely chopped
1  tsp. salt

Saute leeks in 3 tbsp. oil in heavy saucepan. Add red pepper and ½ tsp. salt. Heat 3 tbsp. oil in pan and saute onion until tender, then add beef and cook until color disappears. Add tomato sauce, pepper, 1 tsp. salt and simmer uncovered until the mixture is a thick sauce. Add ⅔ tbsp. mint. Put the lasagne on the bottom of a shallow baking dish. Put leeks over noodles, then add drained yogurt with garlic and salt and the meat sauce. Sprinkle remaining mint on top and bake at 375° F for 15 minutes.

## PORK CHOP CAPER

6   pork chops, cut ¾ inch thick
2   tbsp. flour
1   tsp. salt
¼   tsp. white pepper
2   tbsp. lard or drippings
2   c. 1-inch pieces celery
1   medium onion, finely chopped
¼   cup water
2   tsp. capers, drained
1   clove garlic, crushed
½   pint yogurt

Combine flour, salt and pepper and dredge pork chops. Lightly brown chops in lard or drippings in large frying-pan. Pour off drippings. Add celery, onion, water, capers and garlic and cook slowly, covered, for 45 minutes or until tender. Remove chops and celery to hot platter. Stir a small amount of cooking liquid into yogurt; gradually add mixture to cooking liquid in pan, stirring to blend, and just heat through. 6 servings.

## POLISH MEATBALLS
## WITH YOGURT SAUCE

1½  lb. ground pork
1   egg
½   c. seasoned bread crumbs
½   c. milk
½   c. chopped onion
1½  tsp. salt
½   tsp. marjoram
Pepper
4   tbsp. salad oil

34

1   c. water
1   beef bouillon cube
½   c. yogurt
2   tsp. lemon juice
Mashed potatoes
¼   c. grated Parmesan cheese

Combine pork, egg, bread crumbs, milk, onion, salt, marjoram and pepper; mix until blended. Shape into balls 1½ inches. Roll in 2 tbsp. of flour. Brown in salad oil. Mound in center of 2-qt. casserole. Measure drippings in skillet; add more oil to make 2 tbsp. Stir in remaining flour; gradually stir in water and bouillon cubes. Bring to boil; remove. Add yogurt and lemon juice. Spoon mashed potatoes around meatballs. Sprinkle potatoes with cheese. Pour yogurt sauce over meatballs. Bake at 350° F for 1 hour or until potatoes are golden brown. 8 servings.

# CHRISTMAS PORK PIE – FRANCE

2   lb. pork, ground twice
1   c. chicken broth
¼   c. grated onion
salt and pepper to taste
½   tsp. sage
¼   tsp. nutmeg
¼   tsp. ginger
¼   tsp. dry mustard
4   c. unsifted flour
½   c. yogurt
3   eggs
1   c. shortening

Cook meat, broth and onion slowly in pan until done, about 1 hour. Add salt, pepper, sage, nutmeg, ginger and mustard; mix well and set aside. Combine ½ c. flour, yogurt, 2 eggs and ⅛ tsp. salt; mix until smooth. Add shortening and remaining flour; mix until dough can be cut easily with a knife. Roll out and fit into a 9-inch pie pan. Fill with cooled pork mixture, cover with top crust and brush with beaten egg. Bake at 400° F for 35 minutes.

# MEXICAN STYLE YOGURT DINNER

2   lb. bulk pork sausage
1   c. diced onions
1   c. diced green peppers
1   can tomatoes
2   c. uncooked macaroni
2   tbsp. sugar
1   tbsp. chili powder
1   tsp. salt
1   c. yogurt

Brown sausage, onions and green peppers in skillet. Pour off fat. Add tomatoes, macaroni, seasonings and yogurt. Cover and cook slowly on low heat for 10 minutes. Uncover and simmer for 20 minutes. Serve. 6 servings.

# VEAL STROGANOFF

¼   c. flour
1   tsp. salt
¼   tsp. pepper
1   lb. veal, cut into strips
¼   c. salad oil
1   medium onion
½   lb. mushrooms, sliced
½   c. water
1   chicken bouillon cube
1   tsp. paprika
1   c. yogurt
cooked noodles

Combine flour, salt and pepper; coat meat with mixture. Heat oil in large frying pan and brown meat. Add onion and mushrooms. Cook 5 minutes. Add water, bouillon and paprika; bring to boil. Reduce heat and blend in yogurt. Cover and simmer for 15 minutes. Serve over noodles. 4 servings.

# ROLLED VEAL IN YOGURT

1½ lb. veal steak
1   tbsp. onion, minced
1   tbsp. celery, chopped
6   tbsp. butter
1   c. soft bread crumbs
1   tbsp. parsley, minced
½  tsp. salt
½  tsp. paprika
½  tsp. thyme
Flour
4   tbsp. butter
1½ c. yogurt

Cut veal into 6-inch squares. Saute onion and celery in 2 tbsp. of butter. Stir in bread crumbs, parsley, salt, paprika and thyme. Spread veal with bread filling; roll and tie with white string. Dip in flour. Saute in remaining butter until brown. Add yogurt. Simmer for 30 minutes. 6 servings.

# VEAL N' NOODLES

2   tsp. salt
⅓  c. flour
1   tbsp. paprika
4   lb. veal steaks
½  c. oil
2   c. water
1   c. yogurt
cooked noodles

Mix salt, flour and paprika; pound into veal. Keep the excess seasoned flour. Heat oil in pan and brown steaks 10 minutes on each side. Reduce heat and add 1 c. water. Cover and cook until meat is tender, about 1 hour. Add remaining water and flour and stir. Cook 3 minutes. Add yogurt and heat, but do not boil. Serve on noodles. 6 servings.

# YOGURT NUT STEAK WITH LAMB

4   lean lamb steaks, ½ inch thick
2   tbsp. butter
salt and pepper
6   tbsp. dry sherry
1   c. yogurt
⅓   c. finely chopped salted peanuts
2   tbsp. chopped fresh parsley

Trim steaks well; brown on both sides in heavy pan in butter over medium heat. Season with salt and pepper. Reduce heat; add 4 tbsp. sherry. Cover; simmer for 15 minutes or until tender. Remove steaks from pan; keep warm. Add yogurt and remaining sherry to drippings; heat slowly, stirring to blend. Return steaks to pan with nuts, and parsley; cover with sauce from pan. Heat. Serves 4.

# BASIC YOGURT MARINADE

To get that extra touch of flavor into a wide variety of main dishes, make a marinade with two cups of yogurt, lemon juice, salt; place chicken parts or meat into it overnight. You can season if you so desire.

# MARINADE FOR ROAST

1   c. yogurt
2   tbsp. lemon juice
2   tsp. Worcestershire Sauce
2   tsp. celery salt
1   tsp. paprika
2   cloves garlic, finely chopped
2   tsp. salt
¼   tsp. pepper

Combine all ingredients. Marinate roast in mixture for 24 hours. Marinade for 3 to 5 pounds of meat.

# HORSERADISH SAUCE

1   c. yogurt
3   tbsp. horseradish
1   tbsp. orange marmalade
salt to taste

Blend yogurt, horseradish and orange marmalade; add salt. Serve with pot roast.

# Yogurt Main Course Dishes: Fowl

## BAKED CHICKEN IN YOGURT WITH SAUTERNE

8   chicken breasts, split
Seasoned flour
Butter
1   lb. fresh mushrooms
1½  c. yogurt
½   c. Sauterne wine
Pinch of rosemary

Coat chicken in seasoned flour. Brown in butter. Place in covered baking dish. Brown mushrooms in 2 tbsp. fat from chicken. Add yogurt, wine and rosemary. Simmer until sauce is smooth, but do not boil. Pour sauce over chicken and bake at 350° F for 1½ hours. 4 servings.

## YOGURT CHICKEN, SOUTHERN STYLE

1   large fryer
salt and pepper to taste
1   tsp. garlic salt
1   c. yogurt
1   c. flour
2   c. corn oil

Cut chicken into serving pieces; wash and dry. Sprinkle with salt, pepper, and garlic salt; dip in yogurt. Shake in flour in paper bag. Heat oil, add chicken and cook until golden brown. Drain.

# LEMON N' YOGURT CHICKEN

1   4-lb. broiler
3   tbsp. butter
4   lemon slices
salt
¾   tsp. thyme
¼   tsp. pepper
3   tbsp. flour
1   c. cream
½   c. yogurt
¼   c. water
1   egg yolk

Saute chicken in butter but do not brown. Add lemon, salt, thyme and pepper. Cover and simmer until tender. Remove chicken to a covered serving dish and keep it warm. Add flour to pan and stir until smooth. Add cream, yogurt, sherry, water and salt to taste. Cook until thickened. Stir a little sauce into beaten egg yolk; stir egg into sauce. Heat and pour over chicken.

# EAST INDIAN CHICKEN

3   broilers, halved
½   tsp. salt
Juice of 4 limes
2   cloves of garlic, pressed
1   tsp. ginger
1   tbsp. vinegar
½   tbsp. cumin seed, ground
Red pepper
3   tbsp. yogurt
1   tbsp. paprika
Butter

Wash and dry chicken; rub with salt and ¼ of the lime juice. Let stand for 30 minutes. Combine all remaining ingredients except butter into a marinade and rub chicken with it. Place in a covered bowl; refrigerate 12 hours. When ready to cook, rub off excess marinade; place chicken in a flat pan. Bake at 350° F for 40 minutes. Remove; brush with butter. If skin is not bright red put on more paprika.

41

Place chicken under broiler for 19 minutes until crisp—not black.
6 servings.

## YOGURT CHICKEN PAPRIKASH
## AND DUMPLINGS

3   tbsp. shortening or butter
1   c. onion, chopped
1   3-lb. chicken
2   tsp. paprika
½   green pepper
1   tbsp. salt
½   tsp. pepper
Water to cover
2   tbsp. flour
2   c. yogurt

Melt shortening in heavy pan; brown onion. Add chicken, paprika,
green pepper, salt and pepper. Mix well. Add water to cover. Cover
pan and simmer until chicken is tender. Mix flour with yogurt and
milk to form paste, add to chicken and stir. Bring to boil and remove
from heat.

**DUMPLINGS**
3   large eggs
½   tsp. salt
1   tbsp. water
2   c. flour

Beat eggs, salt and water. Add flour slowly until batter is stiff. Drop
by teaspoonful into rapidly boiling salted water. Cook 20 minutes.
Drain well and add to chicken.

## OMAR'S CHELO CON POLLO

2   tbsp. cooking oil
2½ to 3 pound chicken, cut into serving pieces
1   envelope dry onion-mushroom soup mix
1½ c. water
¼   c. seedless raisins

¼   c. slivered almonds
¼   tsp. ground cinnamon
2    to 3 c. hot cooked rice
½   c. plain yogurt
1    tbsp. flour

In large skillet, heat oil and brown chicken well; drain. Stir in onion-mushroom mix blended with water, raisins, almonds, and cinnamon. Bring to a boil, then simmer covered, stirring occasionally, 40 minutes or until chicken is tender. Remove chicken to serving platter arranged with rice and keep warm.

Into skillet, gradually stir in yogurt blended with flour; heat through but do not boil. Serve gravy with chicken and rice; garnish, if desired, with lemon slices and mint. Makes 4 to 6 servings.

## PAKISTANI BAKED CHICKEN

1    small onion
1    small ginger root or ¼ tsp. powdered ginger
1    clove garlic
1    4-lb. roasting chicken
½   tsp. dried ground chili
1½  tsp. salt
1    tsp. black pepper
1    c. yogurt
¼   c. butter

Chop onion and ginger root; mince garlic. Prick chicken with fork. Make a paste of onion, ginger, garlic, chili, salt, black pepper and yogurt. Rub all over surface and inside chicken and allow to stand for 1 hour. Melt butter in baking dish. Place chicken in dish. Roast at 350° F for 2 hours or until tender. Add small amount of water if necessary. 5 servings.

# YOGURT-CHICKEN FRICASSEE

1   5-lb. stewing chicken
3   stalks celery
2   carrots
1   onion
salt
1   qt. yogurt
3   tbsp. flour
1   qt. chicken broth
½   onion, finely chopped
4   tbsp. butter
salt and pepper to taste

Place chicken, celery, carrots, onion and salt in pan with water to cover. Cook until tender. Remove and cool. Strain broth. Saute chopped onion in butter. Add broth and bring to a boil. Combine yogurt and flour and add slowly to broth, stirring constantly. Season to taste with salt and pepper. Simmer for 10 minutes. Remove chicken from bones and add to sauce. Serve over rice. Serves 6.

# MEXICAN CHICKEN IN YOGURT

2   lb. chicken breasts
1   small onion
2   cloves garlic
2   c. yogurt
salt
16  corn tortillas
Oil
1   lb. cheddar cheese, grated
½   green pepper
1   small can green chilis, diced
Hot pepper sauce
Paprika

Cook chicken until tender. Pull meat into bite-sized pieces. Grate onion and garlic into yogurt. Add a little salt. Soften tortillas by quick frying in oil; drain. Wrap chicken and all but 1 c. cheese in tortillas. Put one layer of tortilla rolls in casserole. Sprinkle with green pepper and chilis. Spread with yogurt mixture. Add cheese and a few drops of hot sauce. Repeat layers until all ingredients are used up. End with yogurt. Sprinkle paprika on top. Chill 8 hours. Bake at 350° F for 1 hour. 6 servings.

## CURRIED CHICKEN BREASTS

1    tbsp. flour
6    chicken breasts, skinned
Salt and pepper
1    c. (8 oz.) plain yogurt
1½ to 2 tbsp. curry powder
1    tsp. paprika
3    tbsp. melted butter
1    lemon or lime

Preheat oven to 350⁰ F. Shake 1 tbsp. flour in family size (14" x 20") Brown-IN-Bag and place in two-inch deep roasting pan. Season chicken breasts with salt and pepper; place in single layer in oven bag. Combine remaining ingredients, except lemon or lime, and pour over chicken. Close bag with twist tie; make six half-inch slits in top. Cook 45 minutes, or until tested tender. To serve, squeeze lemon or lime juice over chicken. Serves 5 to 6.

## CHICKEN WING PARTY PLATTER

1    tbsp. flour
3    lbs. chicken wings
Salt
Pepper
1    c. plain yogurt
2    tbsp. curry powder
1    tsp. paprika

Preheat oven to 350⁰ F. Shake 1 tbsp. flour in each of two small (10" x 16") Brown-In-Bags* and place each bag in a two inch deep roasting pan. Cut wings apart at joints. Save wing tip portion for soup or broth. Place remaining two sections of each wing into bags,

*To cook just one round of hot servings, use large size (14" x20") Brown-In-Bag for recipe amounts.

dividing between bags. Season chicken with salt and pepper. Combine yogurt curry powder and paprika; spoon mixture over chicken, dividing between the two bags. Close bags with twist ties; make six half-inch slits in top. Cook one bag for 45 minutes and serve. Reserve other bag to cook and serve mid-way during party. Makes 64 pieces.

## TURKEY PAPRIKA

| | |
|---|---|
| 2 | c. sliced roasted turkey |
| ¼ | c. butter |
| 1 | medium onion, sliced |
| ¼ | c. flour |
| 1 | tsp. salt |
| 2 | c. milk |
| 4 | tsp. paprika |
| 1 | 4-oz. can mushrooms, drained |
| 1 | c. yogurt |
| 1 | tbsp. poppy seed |
| 2 | tbsp. butter |
| 1 | 7-oz. pkg. noodles, cooked |

Melt ¼ c. butter in pan. Add onion and cook until tender. Blend in flour and salt. Remove from heat. Gradually add milk, stirring constantly; cook until thick. Reduce heat and stir in paprika. Add mushrooms and turkey. Simmer 5 minutes. Stir in yogurt and heat. Serve on poppy seed noodles. To make, add poppy seed and butter to drained noodles and toss together. 6 servings.

# YOGURT CHESTNUT DRESSING

1    c. yellow corn meal
1    c. thin yogurt
1    egg
2    tsp. baking powder
1    tsp. soda
salt
1    tbsp. sugar
10   slices bread
15   crackers
6    hard-boiled eggs, chopped
5    c. of broth
1    5-oz. can water chestnuts, chopped
1    tsp. rubbed sage
pepper

Combine meal, yogurt, egg, baking powder, soda, 1 tsp. salt and sugar. Pour into well-greased pan. Bake at 450° F until done. Brown bread slices and crackers; crumble with corn bread. Add eggs, broth, water chestnuts and seasonings. Bake at 400° F for 20 minutes. 12 servings.

# Yogurt Main Course Dishes: Seafood

## BAKED COD WITH YOGURT

2    lb. cod steak or fillet
¼    c. butter
½    c. grated Parmesan cheese
1    c. yogurt

Put fish in a shallow greased baking dish. Melt butter and stir in grated cheese and yogurt. Spoon sauce on fish. Bake at 400° F for 20 minutes or until sauce is golden brown and fish flakes easily with a fork.

## BAKED RED SNAPPER

4    lb. red snapper
salt
2    tbsp. oil
¾    c. chopped celery
½    c. chopped onion
¼    c. oil
1    qt. dry bread crumbs
½    c. yogurt
¼    c. diced peeled lemon
2    tbsp. grated lemon rind
1    tsp. paprika

Clean and rub fish with 1½ tsp. salt and ¼ c. diced peeled lemon. Cook celery and onion in oil until tender. Mix well with remaining ingredients and 1 tsp. salt. Stuff fish cavity; tie together. Bake at 350° F 40 minutes. Baste if fish seems dry. 4 servings.

## BAKED YOGURT FISH FILLET

1    small onion, minced
1    clove garlic, minced
1    tbsp. butter
2    lb. lean fish fillets
salt
pepper
½   c. yogurt
Fresh parsley

Saute onion and garlic in butter until lightly browned. Lay fish fillets in a casserole dish over the onion and garlic. Salt and pepper. Cover fish with yogurt mixed with chopped parsley. Bake at 350° F for 15 minutes or until fish flakes easily. 3 servings.

## BROILED SALMON IN YOGURT SAUCE

4    salmon steaks, cut 1 inch thick
2    tbsp. lemon juice
¼   tsp. salt
pepper to taste
2    tbsp. butter, melted
⅛   tsp. marjoram
Yogurt sauce
Minced parsley
Lemon slices

Wipe fish with damp cloth. Mix lemon juice, salt, pepper, butter and marjoram. Place steaks on cold broiler; brush with lemon juice mixture. Broil 3 to 4 inches below flame until golden brown (20 minutes). Do not turn. Spoon yogurt sauce over fish and sprinkle with parsley. Garnish with lemon slices.

½ c. yogurt
1½ tsp. vinegar
1½ tsp. grated onion
1½ tsp. honey
salt and pepper to taste

Mix ingredients. 4 servings.

# YOGURT / CHEESE FISH

4   pieces fish fillet
salt
Lemon juice
½ c. yogurt
3   tbsp. grated horseradish
4   tbsp. grated Parmesan cheese
Bread crumbs
Pepper to taste

Sprinkle fillets with salt and lemon juice and let stand in refrigerator for several hours. When ready to cook, drain. Place in a buttered baking dish and sprinkle on more lemon juice. Add yogurt and horseradish, then cheese, bread crumbs and pepper. Bake at 350° F for 30 minutes. 4 servings.

# COOL AS A CUCUMBER FISH FILLETS

1   lb. fish fillets, fresh or frozen and thawed
2   tbsp. fresh lemon juice
¼ c. water
1   tsp. salt
⅛ tsp. pepper
⅛ tsp. paprika
¼ tsp. parsley flakes
Cucumber Sauce (recipe follows)

Place regular size (10'' x 16'') Brown-In-Bag in 10x6x2-inch baking dish; arrange fish in single layer in bag. In small bowl, combine remaining ingredients; pour over fish. Close bag with rubber band, string or ¾-inch strip cut from open end of bag; make 6 half-inch slits in top. Micro-cook 4 to 5 minutes, turning dish once, or until fish flakes easily. Serve with Cucumber Sauce. Makes: 3–4 servings.

**CUCUMBER SAUCE**
¾  c. diced, peeled cucumber
1  tbsp. grated lemon rind
2  green onions, sliced
¼  tsp. dill weed
½  c. plain, low fat yogurt

In small bowl combine all ingredients. Refrigerate to develop the flavor.

## SMUGGLER'S COVE FISH SAUCE

1  can (30 oz.) fruit cocktail
2  tbsp. butter or margerine
2  tbsp. all purpose flour
½  tsp. salt
Dash cayenne pepper
1  green onion, including stem, chopped
2  c. plain yogurt
2  tbsp. capers

Drain fruit cocktail. In medium saucepan over low heat melt butter; stir in flour, salt, cayenne pepper and green onion. Gradually stir in ½ c. yogurt, stirring constantly until mixture is thickened and smooth. Remove from heat. Stir in remaining yogurt, capers and fruit cocktail. Serve generously over broiled or baked fish. Serves 6.

## CARAWAY YOGURT CHEESE WITH PICNIC SARDINES

Cheesecloth
1  pkg. (8 oz.) cream cheese, softened
1  tsp. caraway seeds
2  cartons (8 oz. each) plain yogurt
½  tsp. salt
Crispbread or crackers
Picnic Sardines (recipe follows)

51

In medium bowl, beat cream cheese until smooth. Stir in caraway seeds, yogurt and salt; pour into cheesecloth lined strainer. Tie together all corners of cheesecloth. Place strainer over bowl; refrigerate 24 hours, or more, stirring once or twice. Discard liquid that drips into bowl. Transfer to foam cup and refrigerate until you pack it for your picnic. To serve: spread on crispbread; top with picnic sardines; garnish with hard-cooked egg quarters and parsley, if desired. Makes 4 to 6 servings.

### PICNIC SARDINES

2   cans (3¾ oz. *each*) Norway sardines in mustard sauce or tomato sauce
2   tsp. white vinegar
½   tsp. *each* salt, sugar and dill weed
¼   tsp. pepper

In small bowl, mash sardines in their sauce. Stir in vinegar, salt, sugar, dill weed and pepper. refrigerate in foam cup until serving time. Makes 1 cup.

# CRAB CREPES WITH YOGURT

1   clove garlic, minced
2   onions, chopped
2   tbsp. olive oil
1½ No. 2 cans tomatoes
salt
Black pepper
2   cans chili peppers
2   eggs
4   c. milk
2   c. sifted flour
2   c. cooked crab meat
1½ c. yogurt

Saute onions and garlic in olive oil. Add tomatoes, salt and black pepper; simmer for 20 minutes. Add chili peppers cut into strips. Beat eggs; add milk, stir in flour gradually and beat until smooth. Butter a crepe pan and pour in a thin film of batter. Fill each crepe with tomato/pepper mixtue and crab meat. Put crepes in baking dish and cover with a small amount of tomato/pepper mixture and yogurt. Heat in 300° F oven.

# MOULE A LA YOGURT

6    qt. mussels
1    large onion, chopped
½    c. parsley, chopped
**Butter**
6    heaping tbsp. yogurt

Scrape and clean the mussel shells. Saute onion and parsley in butter. Place onion, parsley and mussels in large kettle. Cover with water and boil for about 10 minutes. Uncover; add yogurt and mix with a wooden spoon. Serve steaming hot in individual soup plates. If raw mussels are open or float to the surface of the cleaning water they're not good. 6 servings.

# FANCY SHRIMP

2    tbsp. minced shallots
2    tbsp. butter
1    lb. cleaned shrimp
¼    lb. sliced mushrooms
1    tsp. salt
⅛    tsp. black pepper
3    tbsp. chili sauce
1⅔ c. water
1⅓ c. minute rice
1    c. yogurt
1    tbsp. flour
1    tbsp. chives

Saute shallots in butter. Add shrimp and mushrooms. Saute and stir until shrimp are pink. Combine salt, pepper, chili sauce and water. Add to shrimp mixture. Bring to boil and stir in rice. Cover and simmer 15 minutes. Combine yogurt and flour; add to rice. Heat gently. Pour into serving dish, sprinkle with chives. Serves 4.

# Yogurt Main Course Dishes: Casseroles

## NOODLE AND HAM CASSEROLE

¼ lb. butter
1 egg
1 c. yogurt
½ lb. egg noodles, cooked
½ lb. cooked diced ham
½ tsp. salt
¼ tsp. pepper
¼ tsp. paprika

Grease 2-qt. casserole with 2 tbsp. butter. Cream remaining butter; add egg and yogurt. Mix well. Stir in cooked noodles, ham, salt, pepper and paprika. Pour into greased casserole. Bake at 350° F for 1 hour. 4 servings.

## EGG AND YOGURT CASSEROLE

9 hard-cooked eggs, halved
6 tbsp. soft butter
1 tsp. grated onion
4 tsp. minced parsley
1⅔ tsp. salt
Dash of pepper
1 c. yogurt
½ c. dry bread crumbs

Remove yolks from eggs; mash. Blend with 3 tbsp. butter, onion, parsley, mustard, salt and pepper. Fill egg whites with mixture and place cut side down in shallow casserole. Cover with yogurt, sprinkle with crumbs. Dot with butter. Bake at 350° F for 25 minutes. 6 servings.

## CHEESE AND CHILI CASSEROLE

| ¾ | lb. Jack cheese |
| 3 | c. yogurt |
| 2 | c. peeled, diced green chilies |
| 3 | c. cooked rice |
| salt and pepper to taste | |
| ½ | c. grated cheddar cheese |

Cut Jack cheese in strips. Thoroughly mix yogurt and chilies. Butter casserole. Put in a layer of rice; add salt and pepper, then a layer of yogurt, then cheese strips. End with rice. Bake at 350° F for 30 minutes. In the last 5 minutes sprinkle on the cheddar to melt it. 8 servings.

## YOGURT BEAN CASSEROLE

| 2 | pkg. frozen French-style beans |
| 2 | tbsp. flour |
| 1 | tsp. salt |
| ¼ | tsp. pepper |
| 2 | tbsp. butter |
| 1 | c. yogurt |
| ½ | c. grated sharp cheese |

Cook beans as directed; drain. Add flour, salt, pepper and butter. Mix yogurt with bean mixture and put in a baking dish. Bake at 350° F for 15 minutes. 6 servings.

# RUSSIAN MUSHROOM MEAT CASSEROLE

1½   lb. round steak
½    lb. pork
Butter
1¼   tsp. salt
½    tsp. pepper
3    medium onions, thinly sliced
1    c. mushrooms, sliced, reserve liquid
1    tsp. capers
1    c. cooked rice
2    c. yogurt
2    bay leaves, crushed
Paprika
Green peppers, cut into rings

Trim fat from meat, grind meat coarsely. Brown meat lightly in 3 tbsp. butter. Season with salt and pepper. In another pan fry onions and mushrooms in 2 tbsp. of butter. Add capers. Spread half the meat in buttered 11 x 7 x 1½ inch baking dish. Add ½ c. cooked rice, spreading thinly. Top with onions and mushrooms. Add another layer of rice and the remaining meat. Melt 2 tbsp. butter in pan in which meat was browned. Add yogurt, reserved liquid from mushrooms and crushed bay leaves. Heat, do not boil. Pour topping over casserole, sprinkle with paprika. Bake in 350° F oven for 30 minutes.

# YOGURT MOUSSAKA

2½   lb. eggplant
salt
1    small onion, chopped
2    tbsp. olive oil
2    lb. ground lamb or beef
1    tsp. paprika
¼    tsp. pepper
Flour
4    medium fresh tomatoes, sliced
1    c. yogurt
4    egg yolks

Peel and slice eggplant into ¼-inch slices. Sprinkle with salt and let stand for 1 hour. Saute onion in oil. Add meat, 2 tsp. of salt, paprika and pepper; brown. Pour excess fat into another skillet. Dip eggplant slices into flour; brown in hot fat drained from meat. Arrange alternate layers of meat mixture and eggplant in a 3-qt. casserole. Top with tomato slices. Bake at 350° F for 1 hour. Stir yogurt and egg yolks into ½ c. flour and mix well. Pour over casserole. Bake for 15 minutes longer or until browned. 6 servings.

## CHEESE YOGURT ROMANOFF

| 2 | 8-oz. pkg. egg noodles, cooked |
| 3 | c. large-curd cottage cheese |
| 2 | tsp. Worcestershire Sauce |
| 2 | cloves garlic, minced |
| 1 | bunch scallions, finely chopped |
| 2 | c. yogurt, creamy |
| ½ | tsp. Tabasco Sauce |
| 1 | c. grated cheddar cheese |

Combine all ingredients except grated cheese. Pour in buttered casserole and sprinkle with grated cheese. Bake at 350° F for 25 minutes. 16 servings.

## CHEESE AND BEEF CASSEROLE

| 1½ | lb. ground beef |
| 1 | medium onion, chopped |
| 1 | clove garlic, minced |
| 2 | tbsp. butter |
| 1 | tsp. salt |
| ⅛ | tsp. pepper |
| 2 | 8-oz. cans tomato sauce |
| 1 | c. cottage cheese |
| 1 | 8-oz. pkg. cream cheese |
| ¼ | c. yogurt |
| ¼ | c. chopped green pepper |
| ¼ | c. chopped scallions |
| 1 | 8-oz. pkg. noodles, cooked and drained |

Saute onion and garlic in butter until onion is soft. Add ground beef and brown. Add salt, pepper and tomato sauce; simmer slowly. Combine cottage cheese, cream cheese, yogurt, green pepper and scallions. Place half of cooked noodles in a greased 3-qt. casserole. Top with cheese mixture and then remaining noodles. Pour meat mixture over the top. Bake at 350° F for 30 minutes. 8 servings.

## VEAL YOGURT SUPREME

1½   lb. veal steak or veal stew meat, cubed
1   onion, chopped
2   tbsp. butter or margarine
1   can mushroom soup
1   small can mushrooms
1   c. yogurt
1   green pepper, diced
salt and pepper to taste
1   12-oz. pkg. cooked noodles
2   c. grated sharp cheese
Buttered bread crumbs

Saute veal and onion in butter. Add small amount of water; simmer until tender. Add soup, mushrooms, yogurt, green pepper, salt and pepper. Blend well. Place alternate layers of noodles, veal mixture and cheese in long casserole. Top with crumbs. Bake at 350° F for 45 minutes. 8 servings.

## GREEN NOODLE AND VEAL YOGURT

1   lb. veal steak
1   c. flour
1   tsp. salt
1   tsp. pepper
Paprika
1   c. hot water
1   c. yogurt
4   oz. green noodles
¼   c. butter
2   tbsp. poppy seed
½   c. almonds, toasted
10½ oz. cream or evaporated milk

Cut meat into serving pieces; dredge in flour, salt, pepper and paprika. Brown in hot fat; add water. Cover and simmer 1 hour. Add yogurt just before serving and heat, but do not boil. Cook noodles; drain. Add butter, poppy seed, almonds and cream. Layer meat and noodles in casserole. Bake at 350° F for 30 minutes. 4 servings.

## BACON AND YOGURT CASSEROLE

½   lb. bacon
1   c. raw macaroni, cooked
1   c. grated Jack cheese
½   c. yogurt
¼   c. milk
¼   tsp. salt
1   tsp. Worcestershire Sauce
1   tbsp. chopped pimento
2   tbsp. chopped green pepper
1   2-oz. can of mushrooms

Cook bacon over low heat until crisp. Drain and crumble. Combine all ingredients. Place in 1-qt. casserole and bake at 350° F for 30 minutes. 4 servings.

## ENCHILADA BAKE

½   c. dried beans, cooked
1   onion, chopped
1   clove garlic, minced
5   to 6 mushrooms, sliced
1   green pepper, chopped
1½   c. cooked tomatoes
1   tbsp. chili powder
1   tsp. ground cumin
salt to taste
½   c. red wine
6   to 8 corn tortillas
½   c. Monterey Jack Cheese
⅓   c. cottage cheese
⅓   c. yogurt
**Black olives (optional)**

Saute onion, mushrooms and pepper. Add the tomatoes, spices, salt and wine. Simmer gently about 30 minutes. Add the beans during the last 5 minutes of cooking time.

Combine cottage cheese and yogurt. In an oiled casserole put a layer of tortillas, a layer of sauce, 3 tbsp. grated cheese, and approximately 3 tbsp. of the cheese-yogurt mixture. Repeat until all the ingredients are used, ending with a layer of sauce. Garnish with black olives. Bake at 350° F for 15 to 20 minutes. Makes 4 servings.

# CRAB CASSEROLE

| | |
|---|---|
| 1 | 7½-oz. can crab |
| 1 | tbsp. lemon juice |
| 2 | c. shell macaroni |
| 1 | 8-oz. pkg. cream cheese (room temperature) |
| ½ | c. yogurt |
| ½ | c. cottage cheese |
| ¼ | tsp. garlic powder |
| ½ | tsp. salt |
| ¼ | tsp. pepper |
| ¼ | c. sliced green onion |
| 2 | medium tomatoes, thinly sliced |
| 1 | c. grated cheddar cheese |

Drain crab; slice into bite-sized pieces. Sprinkle with lemon juice. Cook macaroni in boiling salted water until tender; drain. Add cream cheese to hot macaroni; toss to coat. Add yogurt, cottage cheese and seasonings. Put in a buttered 2-qt. baking dish. Sprinkle onion over macaroni. Spread with layer of crab, then a layer of sliced tomatoes. Sprinkle tomatoes with salt and pepper. Top with grated cheese. Bake at 350° F for 30 minutes. Serves 6.

# *Yogurt Salads:*
# *Main Dish*
# *Side Dishes*

## STUFFED GREEN CHILIS WITH YOGURT

2    ripe avocados, peeled and mashed
1    tbsp. lemon juice
¼    tsp. salt
¼    tsp. pepper
¼    tsp. chili powder
1    tbsp. grated onion
2    small cans green chilis, drained
Lettuce
Tomato wedges
Yogurt
Paprika

Combine avocados, juice, salt, pepper, chili powder and onion. Mix well and stuff each chili with mixture. Serve 2 chilis on shredded lettuce with tomato wedges and top with yogurt. Sprinkle paprika over all. 6 servings.

# COCONUT CHIP CHICKEN SALAD WITH YOGURT AND PEACHES

| | |
|---|---|
| 1 | 1-lb. 13-oz. can cling peach halves |
| ¼ | c. mayonnaise |
| ¼ | c. yogurt |
| ½ | tsp. curry powder |
| ½ | c. drained finely chopped chutney |
| 2½ | c. diced cooked chicken |
| 1 | c. chopped celery |
| ½ | c. toasted coconut chips |
| salt to taste | |
| Salad greens | |

Chill peaches. Blend mayonnaise, yogurt, curry powder and chutney. Add chicken, celery and coconut. Toss lightly, add salt to taste. Drain peaches and arrange on top of salad greens. Top each half with chicken salad. 6 servings.

# GINGER/YOGURT CHICKEN SALAD

| | |
|---|---|
| 3 | c. diced cooked chicken |
| 1½ | c. celery, chopped |
| 1½ | tsp. salt |
| ¼ | tsp. pepper |
| 3 | tbsp. candied ginger, chopped |
| 1½ | tsp. honey |
| 1½ | c. yogurt |
| Paprika | |
| Lettuce | |

Combine chicken, celery, salt and pepper. Chill for 2 hours. Just before serving combine honey, ginger and yogurt. Stir half of this into the chicken. Put on a lettuce bed and top with remaining ginger.

# WINTER GARDEN SALAD

| | |
|---|---|
| 1 | envelope (1 tbsp.) unflavored gelatin |
| ½ | c. water |
| 2 | tsp. salt |

½ tsp. white pepper
2 tbsp. grated onion
¼ c. lemon juice
1 c. diced cucumber
½ c. *each* diced green pepper and pimientos
1 c. thinly sliced celery
2 c. cooked rice
1 carton (8 oz.) yogurt (1 c.)
¼ c. mayonnaise

Soften gelatin in water. Place over low heat and dissolve. Add salt, pepper, grated onion, and lemon juice. Chill until thickness of egg white. Beat until light and fluffy. Fold in vegetables, rice, yogurt, and mayonnaise. Turn into a 1-qt. greased mold. Chill until firm. Garnish with thin slices of cucumber and ripe olives, if desired. Makes 6 servings.

## PICNIC SALAD

2 15-oz. cans kidney beans, drained
4 hard-boiled eggs, diced
½ c. onion, chopped
1 c. celery, diced
⅔ c. chopped sweet pickles
1 c. sharp cheddar cheese
1 c. yogurt

Mix beans, eggs, onion, celery, pickle and cheese. Add yogurt and toss. Serve on lettuce. 10 servings.

## SLIM KIM SPECIAL

1½ c. melba toast crumbs
3 tbsp. melted butter
1 (17 oz.) can cling peach slices
4 8-oz. containers low fat unflavored yogurt (total: 32 oz.)
¼ tsp. grated lemon rind
2 tbsp. sugar
1 envelope plain gelatin
few grains of salt
Fresh or canned fruits for garnish

Combine crumbs and butter and put into buttered 10-inch pie pan. Drain peaches, saving syrup. In blender, whirl peaches, yogurt, lemon rind, sugar and salt. Soften gelatin in reserve ½ c. peach syrup, then heat over hot water (to liquify) and quickly blend into yogurt-peach mixture. Chill mixture to soft peak stage and pile into crumb shell. Chill to set. To serve, cut into wedges and place on salad greens for entree salad; garnish with fresh or canned fruits. Makes 1 large (10 inch) pie. About 8 servings.

## CAULIFLOWER AND YOGURT SALAD

1    small head cauliflower, chopped
3    tbsp. onion, chopped
1    large tomato, chopped
¼    green pepper, chopped

### YOGURT DRESSING
½    c. yogurt
4    tsp. vinegar
1    tbsp. sugar
Dash of salt

Mix cauliflower, onion, tomato and green pepper. Stir yogurt and vinegar together and add sugar and salt. Mix everything together. 4 servings.

## GREEK RICE SALAD

1    can (30 oz.) fruit cocktail
3    to 4 cup cooked instant rice
1    pkg. (12 oz.) frozen chopped spinach*
4    hard boiled eggs, chopped
2    tbsp. mayonnaise
1    tsp. salt
2    tbsp. mustard
1    tbsp. olive oil
3    tbsp. instant minced onion
2    tbsp. plain yogurt
2    tsp. dried or fresh mint

*If fresh spinach is available use one bunch, chopped and uncooked.

2     tbsp. wine vinegar
1     can (4 oz.) pimientos, chopped
**Mint sprigs for garnish**

Drain fruit cocktail. In large bowl combine rice, spinach and eggs; add mayonnaise, salt, mustard, olive oil, onion, yogurt, mint, vinegar and pimientos. Add fruit cocktail and garnish with mint sprig. Serves 6–8.

## RUSSIAN SALAD

2     c. pickled beets
2     or 3 cucumbers
2     c. yogurt
2     tbsp. chopped chives
salt and pepper
2     tbsp. snipped fresh dill.

Drain beets; dry thoroughly on paper towel and cut into strips. Peel and slice cucumbers. Combine yogurt, chives, salt and pepper to taste. Pour over beets and cucumbers, tossing lightly. Chill. Toss again before serving and sprinkle with dill. 6 servings.

## YOGURT SLAW WITH RED CABBAGE

3     c. red cabbage, shredded
¼     c. parsley, chopped
2     tbsp. vinegar
1     tsp. sugar
½     tsp. salt
2     tbsp. capers
1     tbsp. onion
½     c. yogurt

Combine all ingredients. Mix well. 6 servings.

# RED AND GREEN SALAD

2 tbsp. bacon drippings
2 tsp. flour
2 tsp. sugar
½ tsp. salt
1 tsp. dry mustard
Dash cayenne pepper
1 egg
¼ c. vinegar
¼ c. milk
1 c. yogurt
3 c. green cabbage, shredded
3 c. red cabbage, shredded
¾ c. scallions, sliced
6 strips of bacon, cooked and crumbled

Blend bacon drippings, flour, sugar, salt, dry mustard and pepper. Beat egg and vinegar together; add to mixture in skillet. Cook over low heat until smooth and thick, stirring constantly. Combine milk and yogurt. Stir into thickened mixture. Chill. Pour over cabbage, onions and bacon. 8 servings.

# HEARTY BEAN SALAD WITH
# SWEET-SOUR YOGURT DRESSING

1 can (16 oz.) kidney beans, drained
2 hard-cooked eggs, chopped
½ c. chopped celery
¼ c. chopped sweet pickle
¼ tsp. salt

### DRESSING
2 tsp. sugar
2 tsp. wine vinegar
½ tsp. salt
½ tsp. prepared mustard
½ tsp. Worchestershire sauce
Dash pepper
½ c. plain yogurt

For dressing, combine sugar, vinegar, salt, mustard, Worchestershire sauce and pepper. Add yogurt. Chill. For salad, combine beans, eggs, celery, onion, pickle and salt. Add desired amount of dressing; toss lightly. Chill. 4 servings.

## MOLDED YOGURT AND CUCUMBER SALAD

| | |
|---|---|
| 2 | envelopes of gelatin |
| ¼ | c. cold water |
| ½ | c. boiling water |
| ¼ | c. sugar |
| ½ | c. cold water |
| ½ | c. vinegar |
| 2 | tsp. salt |
| ¾ | c. radishes, sliced |
| ¾ | c. cucumbers, peeled and sliced |
| ½ | c. green onions, chopped |
| ½ | tsp. dill seed |
| ¾ | c. yogurt |
| ¼ | c. mayonnaise |
| ¼ | tsp. salt |
| 1 | tsp. vinegar |

Soften gelatin in cold water; add boiling water and sugar. Blend remaining cold water, ½ c. vinegar and 1 tsp. salt; add to gelatin mixture. Add radishes, cucumbers, onion and dill seed. Let set until firm. Combine yogurt, mayonnaise, ¼ tsp. salt and 1 tsp. vinegar. Serve sour cream mixture over gelatin mixture.

# ARTICHOKE SEAFOOD SALAD

| | |
|---|---|
| 6 | artichokes |
| salt | |
| ¼ | lb. fresh mushrooms |
| ¼ | c. chopped green onions |
| ½ | c. chopped cucumbers |
| 2 | tbsp. olive oil |
| 6 | oz. king crab meat |
| ½ | lb. shrimp, chopped |
| 2 | hard boiled eggs |
| ½ | c. mayonnaise |
| ½ | c. yogurt |
| 2 | tbsp. fresh dill or 1 tsp. dill weed |
| ⅛ | tsp. white pepper |
| 2 | tbsp. lemon juice |

Prepare artichokes by washing, cutting off stems and trim sharp tips off ends. Boil gently for 35 to 45 minutes until outside leaves can be pulled off easily. Remove the fuzzy choke by spreading leaves and using a metal spoon. Saute mushrooms and onions in oil until soft. In a bowl, combine mushroom and onions with cucumbers, crab, shrimp, eggs, mayonnaise, yogurt, dill, 1 tsp. salt, pepper and lemon juice. Chill. Fill artichokes with salad. 6 servings.

# CRAB LOUIS SALAD

| | |
|---|---|
| 3 | cans crab |
| 6 | c. shredded lettuce |
| 2 | hard-boiled eggs, diced |
| 2 | tbsp. chopped chives |
| 2 | medium tomatoes, peeled and quartered |
| 1⅓ | c. mayonnaise |
| ⅓ | c. yogurt |
| ½ | c. chili sauce |
| 2 | tbsp. horseradish |
| 4 | tsp. lemon juice |
| 1 | tsp. salt |
| ¼ | tsp. freshly ground black pepper |
| ⅓ | c. chopped scallions |
| 2 | tbsp. chopped capers |
| ¾ | tsp. Worcestershire sauce |

Flake crab into a large salad bowl. Add lettuce and mix. Sprinkle with eggs and chives. Garnish with tomato. Combine remaining ingredients for dressing. Pour dressing over salad and mix. 5 servings.

## SHRIMP CURRY SALAD

| | |
|---|---|
| 4 | lb. cooked shrimp |
| 2 | tbsp. lemon juice |
| ½ | tbsp. grated onion |
| 1½ | tbsp. curry powder |
| 6 | tbsp. yogurt |
| 1 | c. mayonnaise |
| 1 | c. melon balls |
| ½ | c. celery, chopped |
| ½ | c. pineapple chunks |
| French dressing | |

Combine shrimp, lemon juice, onion and salt; chill overnight. Mix curry powder, yogurt and mayonnaise. Let stand for a few hours. Marinate melon balls, celery and pineapple chunks in French dressing for several hours. One hour before serving, combine ingredients and chill. 8 servings.

## HERRING SALAD

| | |
|---|---|
| 2 | salt herring, skinned, filleted and cut into small pieces |
| 2 | c. canned beets, cubed |
| 2 | c. cold boiled potatoes, diced |
| ½ | c. onions, minced |
| 1 | c. tart apples, chopped |
| ½ | c. dill pickles, chopped |
| ½ | c. English walnuts, chopped |
| 1 | c. mayonnaise |
| 1 | tsp. prepared mustard |
| Salt | |
| ½ | tsp. black pepper |
| 5 | tbsp. vinegar |
| ½ | tsp. sugar |
| ½ | c. yogurt |

Combine herring, beets, potatoes, onions, apples, pickles and walnuts. Toss. Combine remaining ingredients, add to herring and toss. Let stand overnight. When ready to serve add more yogurt if it seems dry.

## YOGURT ICEBERG SALAD

| | |
|---|---|
| 1 | head western iceberg lettuce |
| 2 | tomatoes |
| 1 | cucumber |
| 1 | container (8 oz.) plain yogurt |
| 2 | tbsp. finely chopped onion |
| ½ | tsp. minced garlic |
| 1 | tsp. seasoned salt |
| ½ | tsp. sugar |
| ¼ | tsp. oregano, crumbled |
| ¹⁄₁₆ | tsp. white pepper |
| 2 | hard-cooked eggs |

Core, rinse and thoroughly drain lettuce; chill in plastic crisper or disposable plastic bag. Rinse and chill tomato and cucumber. Combine yogurt with onion, garlic, salt, sugar, oregano and pepper; chill. When ready to serve, remove outside lettuce leaves; cut lettuce into crosswise slices, then into bite-size chunks to measure 1 quart. Arrange lettuce leaves on a chilled platter and top with lettuce chunks. Slice tomato and cucumber and half eggs. Arrange over lettuce. Serve with Yogurt Dressing. Makes 4 generous servings.

## HAM AND FRUIT ICEBERG PLATE

| | |
|---|---|
| 1 | head western iceberg lettuce |
| 16 | thin slices cooked ham |
| 1 | red-skinned apple, cut in thin wedges |
| 1 | California avocado, cut in slices |
| ½ | c. plain yogurt |
| 2 | tbsp. tarragon vinegar |
| ¾ | tsp. seasoned salt |
| ½ | tsp. onion powder |
| ½ | tsp. prepared mustard |
| ½ | tsp. sugar |
| ¼ | tsp. tarragon, crushed |
| ⅛ | tsp. pepper |

Core, rinse and thoroughly drain lettuce; chill in plastic bag or lettuce "crisp-it". Shortly before serving, shred 1½ quarts lettuce and divide among 4 chilled salad plates. Top each with 4 ham slices (folded or rolled), apple wedges and avocado slices. Combine all remaining ingredients, and mix well. Serve on salads. Makes 4 servings.

## SPRINGTIME SIDE SALAD

| | |
|---|---|
| 1 | head western iceberg lettuce |
| 12 | cooked spears fresh asparagus, *or* |
| 1 | can (14½ oz.) asparagus spears, drained |
| 6 | radish roses |
| ½ | pint plain yogurt |
| 1 | tbsp. minced or freeze-dried chives |
| 2 | tsp. bottled mixed salad seasonings |
| 1 | tsp. sugar |
| ½ | tsp. salt |

Core, rinse and drain lettuce; store in refrigerator in disposable plastic bag or plastic crisper. Cut head crosswise into 1-inch slices; cut 3 center slices into halves. (Store remaining lettuce for use another time). Top half-slices with asparagus spears, place each on salad plate and trim with radish. For dressing, blend yogurt, chives, salad seasonings, sugar and salt. Spoon a strip of the dressing across each salad; serve them as a dinner side salad or for a first course. Makes 6 servings.

## APPLE/YOGURT SLAW

| | |
|---|---|
| 1 | c. yogurt |
| 2 | tbsp. lemon juice |
| 2 | tbsp. vinegar |
| 2 | tbsp. sugar |
| 1 | tsp. salt |
| ¼ | tsp. pepper |
| 1 | tbsp. dry mustard |
| 1 | large stalk celery, chopped |
| 2 | c. shredded cabbage |
| 1 | c. shredded carrots |
| 2 | large apples, chopped |
| ⅓ | c. raisins |

71

Combine yogurt, lemon juice, vinegar, sugar, salt, pepper and dry mustard; beat until smooth. Mix celery, cabbage, carrots, apples and raisins and mix in yogurt. Chill and serve. 8 servings.

# SWISS CHEESE SALAD

½    lb. Swiss cheese
6    hard-boiled eggs
¾    c. yogurt
1½   tsp. mustard
1    tsp. horseradish
1    tsp. salt
1    tsp. caraway seed

Cut cheese in small cubes and chop eggs. Combine and toss with yogurt and seasonings. Arrange on lettuce. 4 servings.

# FRUIT SALAD

4    c. yogurt
¼    c. honey
1    small can Mandarin oranges
1    No. 2 can pineapple chunks
3    tart apples, unpeeled
4    ripe bananas
2    c. seedless grapes
1    c. pine nuts
¾    c. shredded coconut

Combine yogurt and honey. Drain oranges and pineapple and reserve pineapple juice. Cut apples and bananas into small pieces and dip into pineapple juice (prevents discoloring). Combine oranges, pineapple, apples and bananas with grapes, pine nuts and coconut. Add yogurt and toss lightly. Serve on lettuce. 10 servings.

# BANANA YOGURT SALAD

2    c. diced bananas
1    c. chopped apples
1    c. fruit cocktail
¼    c. raisins
¼    c. yogurt

Combine ingredients and toss with yogurt. Serve on bed of lettuce. 4 servings.

# COLD RASPBERRY SALAD

1    3-oz. pkg. raspberry gelatin
¾    c. boiling water
1    small pkg. frozen raspberries
1    small can crushed pineapple with juice
1    c. yogurt

Dissolve gelatin in boiling water. Add frozen raspberries. Stir and add pineapple with juice. Place half of mixture in 8-inch square pan. Chill until thickened. Spoon yogurt over gelatin, cover with remaining gelatin. Chill until firm. 6 servings.

# Yogurt Salad Dressings

## BASIC YOGURT DRESSING

1    c. creamy yogurt
2    tbsp. white vinegar
1    tbsp. onion, minced
¼    tsp. sugar
¼    tsp. salt
Black pepper

Combine all ingredients. Good for slaw or green salad.

## YOGURT EGG DRESSING

½    c. sugar
1    tsp. dry mustard
1    tsp. salt
¼    tsp. celery seed
1    tbsp. flour
½    c. vinegar
1    c. yogurt
1    tbsp. butter
2    beaten eggs

Mix flour, sugar, salt, mustard and celery seed. Add vinegar, yogurt and butter. Cook gently in double boiler until thickened. Pour mixture over beaten eggs. Return to double boiler and cook until it reaches consistency of soft custard. Cool. Use with coleslaw.

# AVOCADO DRESSING

1    3-oz. pkg. cream cheese, softened
1    clove garlic, mashed
½    green pepper, chopped
2    avocados, chopped
1    c. yogurt
salt and pepper
2    tbsp. mayonnaise

Mash cream cheese and mix in garlic and green pepper. Add remaining ingredients and mix well. Chill and serve.

# BLUE CHEESE DRESSING

⅓    c. mayonnaise
⅓    c. crumbled blue cheese
1    c. plain yogurt

In small bowl, mix mayonnaise and blue cheese. Fold in yogurt. Cover and chill until serving time. Serve with salad greens or with raw vegetables as a dip. Makes about 1½ cups.

# CHEESE AND HONEY DRESSING

1    3-oz. pkg. cream cheese
¼    tsp. salt
2    tbsp. honey
¼    c. yogurt

Mix all ingredients in small bowl and chill. Good for fruit salad.

# ANCHOVY AND CHIVE DRESSING

1    c. mayonnaise
2    tbsp. tarragon vinegar
1    tbsp. lemon juice
1    clove garlic, pressed
¼    c. chopped chives
2    tbsp. minced parsley
½    c. yogurt
1    2-oz. can anchovies, well mashed

Place ingredients in a bowl in the order given. Mix well, cover and re-frigerate for a day.

## SHERRY PAPRIKA SALAD DRESSING

3    oz. Roquefort cheese
1    3-oz. pkg. cream cheese, softened
1    c. creamy yogurt
¼    c. sherry
1    tbsp. grated onion
½    tsp. salt
¼    tsp. paprika
2    drops Tabasco

Crumble Roquefort cheese into bowl and blend cream cheese until smooth. Add remaining ingredients. Cover and store in refrigerator.

## BLEU CHEESE DRESSING

1    qt. mayonnaise
1    clove garlic, pressed
1    3-oz. pkg. bleu cheese
½    c. whipping cream
½    c. yogurt

Mix all ingredients well. Chill and refrigerate. 5 cups.

## THOUSAND ISLAND DRESSING

⅓    c. mayonnaise
¼    c. chili sauce
2    tbsp. chopped pimiento-stuffed olives
1    tbsp. chopped onion
1    tbsp. chopped green pepper
2    tsp. chopped parsley
1    c. plain yogurt

In small bowl, mix mayonnaise with chili sauce, olives, onion, green pepper and parsley. Fold in yogurt. Cover and chill until serving time. Serve as a dressing for salad greens or as a sandwich spread (in place of butter). Makes about 1⅔ cups.

## CRAB LOUIS DRESSING

1      c. mayonnaise
¼      c. yogurt
¼      c. chili sauce
¼      c. scallions, chopped
1      tsp. lemon juice
salt

Combine mayonnaise, yogurt, chili sauce, onion and lemon juice. Salt to taste. 2 cups.

## VERSATILE HERB DRESSING

⅓      c. mayonnaise
1      tsp. sugar
¾      tsp. chopped chives
½      tsp. basil leaves
½      tsp. garlic powder
½      tsp. onion salt
¼      tsp. oregano leaves
1      c. plain yogurt

In small bowl, mix mayonnaise with sugar, chives and seasonings. Fold in yogurt. Cover and chill until serving time. Serve as a dressing for salad greens or cold cooked vegetables; spoon over sliced tomatoes just before serving, or serve as a sauce for beef fondue. Makes about 1⅓ cups.

# Vegetables With Yogurt

## SPANISH ONION PIE

4    Spanish onions, chopped fine
Bacon fat
3    eggs
1    egg yolk, beaten
1    c. yogurt
6    pieces bacon, cooked and crumbled
salt
pepper
¾    tsp. caraway seed
1    9-inch unbaked pastry shell

Fry onions in fat until they are transparent. Combine eggs and yogurt and mix. Add the rest of the ingredients and pour into pastry shell. Bake at 375° F for 35 minutes. 6 servings.

## GREEN PEAS IN YOGURT

1    c. mushrooms
2    tbsp. butter
1    10-oz. pkg. peas
3    scallions, cut lengthwise and in 2½-inch lengths
2    tbsp. water
¾    tsp. salt
pepper
½    c. yogurt
1    tbsp. flour

Saute mushrooms in butter; add peas, scallions, water, salt and pepper. Mix yogurt and flour well and stir into peas. Heat, but do not boil. 4 servings.

## POTATOES AU PRINTEMPS

1½  lb. new potatoes
2    tbsp. chopped scallions
½    c. chopped cucumber
2    tbsp. sliced radishes
1    tsp. salt
pepper
½    c. yogurt
2    tbsp. chopped green pepper

Peel potatoes and cook until tender. Drain. Combine the rest of the ingredients and heat; do not boil. Pour over hot potatoes. 4 servings.

## YOGURT SCALLOPED TOMATOES

1    No. 2½ can tomatoes, drained
1    c. chopped onion
½    c. cheese cracker crumbs
1½   tsp. sugar
½    tsp. salt
¾    c. yogurt
3    slices bread, cubed and toasted
1    tbsp. melted butter

Break tomatoes up and put in a buttered 1½-quart casserole with ½ c. onion, cracker crumbs, sugar and salt. Cover with the rest of the onion and top with yogurt. Sprinkle bread crumbs over yogurt and dot with butter. Bake at 325° F for 20 minutes or until hot. 6 servings.

# BAKED ZUCCHINI IN YOGURT

6    zucchini
¾    c. yogurt
1    c. grated cheddar cheese
1    tbsp. butter
½    tsp. salt
3    tbsp. bread crumbs
2    tbsp. grated Parmesan

Slice squash ½ inch thick. Steam until tender. Place in 1-quart casserole. Combine yogurt, cheddar cheese, butter and salt. Heat until well blended and pour over squash. Combine bread crumbs and cheese and sprinkle over casserole. Bake at 375° F for 10 minutes.

# SPINACH DELIGHT

1    lb. fresh spinach
1    tbsp. butter
1    tbsp. flour
½    c. yogurt
1    tsp. minced onion
½    tsp. salt
¼    tsp. pepper

Cook spinach until done. Melt butter; blend in flour, add yogurt and stir constantly until thick. Add spinach, onion and salt and pepper. Heat thoroughly but do not boil. 4 servings.

# BAKED ASPARAGUS WITH YOGURT

2    lb. fresh asparagus
⅓    c. yogurt
3    tbsp. melted butter
½    c. soft bread crumbs
½    tsp. basil
½    tsp. salt
½    tsp. paprika

Cook asparagus in salted water until slightly tender. Place in shallow pan. Spread with yogurt. Combine butter, bread crumbs, basil, salt and paprika. Sprinkle over asparagus. Bake at 375° F for 8 to 12 minutes or until bread crumbs are browned. 6 servings.

## HEART OF ARTICHOKE WITH YOGURT AND CUCUMBER

| | |
|---|---|
| 1 | 9-oz. pkg. frozen artichoke hearts |
| 8 | c. broken mixed salad greens |
| ½ | c. sliced radishes |
| 2 | tbsp. herb seasoned croutons |
| ⅓ | c. thin yogurt |
| 3 | tbsp. mayonnaise |
| ½ | c. finely diced peeled cucumber |
| 1 | tbsp. lemon juice |
| ½ | tsp. garlic salt |
| ½ | tsp. sugar |
| ⅛ | tsp. pepper |

Cook artichoke hearts according to package directions; drain. Chill. Place greens in a large bowl; arrange artichoke hearts and radish slices on top. Sprinkle with croutons. Blend yogurt and mayonnaise. Stir in cucumber and lemon juice. Add remaining ingredients. Use half the dressing just before serving and serve the rest with the salad.

## YOGURT AND ALFALFA SPROUTS

| | |
|---|---|
| 1 | c. alfalfa sprouts (or any other sprout) |
| ½ | c. water cress, finely chopped |
| ⅓ | c. chopped walnuts |
| ⅓ | c. plain yogurt |
| ¼ | tsp. mint |
| ⅛ | tsp. salt |
| | Salad greens |

Mix sprouts, water cress and walnuts. Make a dressing with yogurt, mint and salt. Mix with sprouts and serve on salad greens. 3 servings.

# BACON N' BEANS

1    No. 303 can green beans
6    slices bacon
2    tbsp. flour
⅔   c. yogurt
¼   tsp. salt
1    tsp. cider vinegar

Take ⅓ cup of liquid from beans and heat beans in rest of stock. Fry bacon until crisp. Blend flour in drippings and add bean stock, yogurt, salt and vinegar. Cook until thickened, stirring constantly. Drain beans and put in serving dish. Top with yogurt mixture and sprinkle with bacon. 4 servings.

# YOGURT BEETS

1    1-lb. can sliced beets
1    c. yogurt
¼   c. salad dressing
1    tbsp. chopped chives
1    tbsp. lemon juice
½   tsp. brown sugar
¼   tsp. dry mustard

Heat beets; drain. Combine remaining ingredients and add to the beets. Heat slowly; do not boil. 4 servings.

# YOGURT AND CHIVES BROCCOLI

1½  lb. fresh broccoli
1    wedge lemon
1    c. French dressing
1    c. yogurt
1    tbsp. chopped chives

Soak broccoli in cold salted water for 30 minutes. Drain and cut off tough stalk and leaves. Steam until tender. Add the lemon wedge to the water to prevent odor. Marinate in the French dressing for 4 hours. Blend yogurt and chives into dip and serve broccoli cold. 4-6 servings.

# BRUSSELS SPROUTS WITH DILLED YOGURT SAUCE

2    lb. Brussels sprouts or 4 10-oz. pkg frozen Brussels sprouts
3    c. beef bouillon
2    c. yogurt
1    tbsp. chopped fresh dill
White pepper
salt

Cover and cook Brussels sprouts in bouillon until tender. Chill in liquid. Blend remaining ingredients and chill. Drain Brussels sprouts and pour sauce over. 8 servings.

# CABBAGE WITH YOGURT SAUCE

1    med. cabbage cut into six wedges
1    c. yogurt
¼    tsp. salt
½    c. cooking water from cabbage
1    tbsp. chopped chives

Remove core from the cabbage wedges. Cook in boiling salted water for 5 minutes. Cover and cook 8 to 10 minutes longer. Heat yogurt and salt in reserved cabbage water; do not boil. Remove from heat and stir in chives. Pour over wedges. 6 servings.

# CUCUMBER IN YOGURT

1    medium cucumber, sliced
1    tsp. salt
3    tbsp. yogurt
1    tsp. vinegar
1    tsp. sugar
¼    tsp. dill weed

Sprinkle cucumbers with salt and cover with water. Soak. Mix yogurt, vinegar, sugar and dill. Drain cucumber and add dressing. 3 servings.

# EGGPLANT FRITTERS

2    eggs
1    c. thin yogurt
1    tsp. salt
½    tsp. soda
2    tsp. baking powder
1½    c. flour
4    tbsp. corn meal
1    med. eggplant, peeled and cubed

Mix all ingredients except eggplant to make a batter. Then fold eggplant into batter; drop into frying pan in 5-inch pancakes. Turn once. Drain on absorbent paper. 8-10 servings.

# CHEESE EGGPLANT WITH CRUMB TOPPING

1    large eggplant, peeled and cubed
2    tbsp. butter
½    c. hot water
2    tbsp. beef bouillon
1    tsp. oregano
1    tsp. basil
1    c. yogurt
1    tbsp. minced onion
½    tsp. salt
¼    tsp. pepper
¼    c. bread crumbs
2    tbsp. grated Parmesan cheese

Saute eggplant in butter until slightly tender. Combine water, beef bouillon, basil and oregano; pour over eggplant. Simmer, covered, until eggplant is tender and liquid is evaporated. Put in shallow baking dish. Combine yogurt, onions, salt and pepper and pour over eggplant. Sprinkle with crumbs and cheese. Bake at 350° F for 25 minutes or until hot and brown.

# EGGPLANT WITH YOGURT

Eggplant
French dressing

1 clove garlic
**Yogurt with minced chives**

Cut eggplant into ½-inch slices. Marinate in French dressing with garlic for 2 hours. Drain and bake at 450° F for 20 minutes. Remove and spread with yogurt and heat for 5 minutes with door open.

## MUSHROOMS WITH YOGURT SAUCE

| | |
|---|---|
| 2 | lb. fresh mushrooms |
| 4 | tbsp. butter |
| 1 | med. onion |
| 1 | tbsp. flour |
| 8 | oz. yogurt |
| 1 | tsp. salt |
| ½ | tsp. pepper |
| 1 | tbsp. minced parsley |
| 3 | pieces bacon, cooked and crumbled |

Wash mushrooms and use only caps. Slice into quarters if they're large. Saute in butter for 3 minutes. Add onion and simmer covered for 15 minutes. Sprinkle flour over mushrooms and stir. Add yogurt, salt and pepper. Heat but do not boil. Sprinkle with parsley and bacon. 6 servings.

## MUSHROOM PAPRIKASH

| | |
|---|---|
| 1 | lb. fresh mushrooms |
| 2 | tbsp. butter |
| 1 | tsp. lemon juice |
| 2 | tbsp. minced onion |
| 1 | tsp. flour |
| ½ | tsp. salt |
| 1 , | tsp. paprika |
| ½ | c. yogurt |

Wash and slice mushrooms. Saute mushrooms and onions in butter and lemon juice until mushrooms are tender. Combine flour, salt and paprika. Add to the mushrooms. Stir and cook 1 minute. Add yogurt and heat but do not boil. 6 servings.

# COTTAGE CHEESE AND PARMESAN POTATOES

6    med. potatoes
1    c. cottage cheese
1    c. yogurt
2    tbsp. chopped onions
2    tbsp. butter
¼    c. Parmesan cheese

Cook potatoes, cool and mash. Salt and pepper to taste. Add yogurt, cottage cheese and chopped onions. Put in lightly buttered casserole. Dot with butter and sprinkle with Parmesan cheese. 6 servings.

# POTATO SOUFFLE

6    large baking potatoes
Butter
1    c. yogurt
1    egg beaten
1    tsp. salt
⅛    tsp. pepper
10   pieces bacon, cooked and crumbled

Rub potato skins with butter. Bake at 350° F 1 hour, until tender. Cut off tops and scoop out potato. Mash potato with yogurt, ¼ c. butter, egg, salt and pepper. Stir in bacon. Stuff shells. Bake at 400° F for 1 hour until heated through. 6 servings.

# Yogurt Breads, Muffins, Cakes, Cookies & Pies

## BASIC YOGURT BREAD

2    c. milk
½    c. yogurt
1    pkg. active dry yeast
6    c. white flour
2    tbsp. sugar
2    tsp. salt

Scald milk and stir in yogurt. Allow to cool to lukewarm. Add yeast and stir until dissolved. Add 2 c. flour, stirring until mixed. Blend sugar and salt, sprinkle over top of dough. Stir in gently. Cover with damp cloth and let rise for 30 minutes. Punch down and stir in flour until dough is too stiff to stir with a spoon. Turn out on floured board and knead. Work in remaining flour until dough is light and satiny. Break into sections and flour lightly. Fold over and seal. Place half full in bread pans. Grease tops and set in warm place and let rise until doubled (2 hours). Bake 20 minutes at 400° F. Reduce heat to 325° F for 30 minutes. 2 loaves.

# YOGURT RHUBARB BREAD

½    c. shortening
1½   c. brown sugar, firmly packed
1    beaten egg
2    c. sifted all-purpose flour
1    tsp. baking soda
1    c. yogurt
1½   c. cut-up fresh rhubarb
½    c. white sugar
1    tsp. cinnamon

Cream shortening and brown sugar and add an egg. Sift flour, baking soda together and add flour alternately with yogurt. Fold in rhubarb. Pour batter into a greased 9-inch square pan. Sprinkle white sugar and cinnamon on the top.

# ONION BREAD

2    medium onions, chopped
8    tbsp. butter
1¾   tsp. salt
Grind of fresh pepper
2    c. flour
3    tsp. baking powder
¾    c. milk
1    c. thin yogurt
3    egg yolks

Cook onions in 4 tbsp. butter until golden. Season with ½ tsp. salt and fresh pepper. Pour mixture in 13 x 9 inch pan and keep pan warm. Set oven at 450° F. Sift flour, baking powder and ½ tsp. salt 3 times; cut in remaining butter. Stir milk in to make a soft dough, turn out on lightly floured board and knead for 1 minute. Roll dough to ½ inch thickness and place on top of onion mixture. Beat yogurt and egg yolks together and season with salt and pepper. Pour over dough. Bake for 12 to 15 minutes. Serve hot.

# EGG BREAD

1    egg, lightly beaten

1  c. thin yogurt
1  c. cornmeal
1  tsp. grated onion
1  tbsp. melted butter
½  tsp. baking soda dissolved in warm water

Combine ingredients and beat well. Pour into muffin pan. Bake at 425° F for 20 minutes.

## STEAMED BROWN BREAD

1  c. flour
1  c. wheat flour
1  c. corn meal
½  c. sugar
1½  tsp. baking powder
½  c. molasses
1½  c. thin yogurt
2  tbsp. salad oil
1  c. raisins
½  c. nuts

Combine dry ingredients. Stir in molasses and yogurt. Blend in the rest of the ingredients. Fill a greased 2-qt. covered jar (peanut butter jars work well). Set on a rack in large kettle. Pour in boiling water to half the depth of the mold. Cover tightly and steam 3 hours and 30 minutes. Keep water boiling, adding it when needed. Run a spatula around mold to loosen bread and cool on a rack.

## SPANISH CORN BREAD

2  c. cornmeal
⅓  c. melted shortening
½  tbsp. salt
1½  tbsp. honey
2  eggs
½  tsp. baking soda
¾  c. thin yogurt
1  can cream-style corn
1  can chili peppers, chopped
1  c. grated cheese

Mix cornmeal, shortening, salt, honey, eggs, soda and yogurt. Add corn and chili and mix. Pour half of batter into greased iron skillet; pour ½ c. grated cheese over batter. Pour remaining batter into skillet and top with the rest of cheese. Bake for 25 minutes at 475° F.

## IRISH SODA BREAD

| | |
|---|---|
| 2 | c. sifted flour |
| ½ | tsp. baking soda |
| 2 | tsp. baking powder |
| ½ | tsp. salt |
| 1 | tbsp. sugar |
| 3 | tbsp. butter |
| ¼ | c. raisins |
| 2 | tsp. caraway seed |
| 1 | c. thin yogurt |

Sift flour, soda, baking powder, salt and sugar together. Work in butter to make fine meal. Stir in raisins and caraway seed. Add yogurt and mix. Spread dough evenly in a greased 9-inch pie pan. Bake at 350° F for 30 minutes.

## YOGURT AND GRAPE NUT BREAD

| | |
|---|---|
| ½ | c. Grape Nuts |
| 1 | c. thin yogurt |
| ½ | c. sugar |
| 1 | egg |
| 2 | c. flour |
| 2 | tsp. baking powder |
| ½ | tsp. baking soda |
| ½ | tsp. salt |

Soak Grape Nuts in yogurt for 20 minutes. Cream sugar and egg and add Grape Nut mixture. Stir in flour, baking powder, soda and salt. Bake in 350° F oven for 25 minutes.

# WHEAT GERM YOGURT BRAID

8     to 9 cups unsifted flour
¾     c. instant nonfat dry milk solids
5     tsp. salt
1     pkg. active dry yeast
2¾    c. water
1     c. (8 oz.) yogurt
¼     c. honey
2     tbsp. margarine
1     c. wheat germ
1     egg, beaten
Wheat germ for topping

In a large bowl thoroughly mix 3½ c. flour, dry milk solids, salt and undissolved Fleischmann's Active Dry Yeast.

Combine water, yogurt, honey and Fleischmann's margarine in a saucepan. Heat over low heat until liquids are very warm (120°F–130° F). Margarine does not need to melt. Gradually add to dry ingredients and beat 2 minutes at medium speed of electric mixer, scraping bowl occasionally. Add 1 cup flour. Beat at high speed 2 minutes, ·scraping bowl occasionally. Stir in 2 c. wheat germ and enough additional flour to make a stiff dough. Turn out onto lightly floured board; knead until smooth and elastic, about 8 to 10 minutes. Place in greased bowl, turning to grease top. Cover; let rise in warm place, free from draft, until doubled in bulk, about 1 hour.

Punch dough down; divide in half. Divide each half into 3 equal pieces. Shape each into a 16-inch rope. Braid 3 ropes together; pinch ends to seal. Place on greased baking sheet. Repeat with remaining ropes. Cover; let rise in warm place, free from draft, until doubled in bulk, about 1 hour.

Brush with beaten egg and sprinkle with wheat germ. Bake at 350° F for 35 minutes, or until done. Remove from baking sheets and cool on wire racks. Makes 2 loaves.

# PEACHY GINGERBREAD

| | |
|---|---|
| 1 | can (16 oz.) cling peach slices |
| 3 | tbsp. butter |
| ½ | c. light brown sugar, packed |
| ¾ | c. chopped almonds |
| 2½ | c. sifted flour |
| 1½ | tsp. baking soda |
| ½ | tsp. ground cloves |
| 1 | tsp. cinnamon |
| 1 | tsp. ginger |
| ¾ | tsp. salt |
| ½ | c. soft shortening |
| ½ | c. granulated sugar |
| 1 | medium egg, unbeaten |
| 1 | c. molasses |
| ⅔ | c. yogurt |

Drain peaches well, reserving syrup. In 9 x 9 x 2-inch pan melt butter; blend with brown sugar and nuts. Arrange peach slices over mixture.

Sift together flour, soda, cloves, cinnamon, ginger and salt. Cream shortening and sugar until fluffy. Add egg, beat about 4 minutes until light and fluffy. Beat in molasses. Alternately beat in dry ingredients, then yogurt. Pour over peach slices in baking pan. Bake 50 minutes at 350° F (moderate) oven. Cool 10 minutes then invert onto serving platter. Serves 6-9.

# BASIC YOGURT ROLLS

| | |
|---|---|
| 2 | c. yogurt |
| 3 | pkg. yeast |
| ¼ | c. shortening |
| 1 | egg, beaten |
| 7 | c. flour |
| 2 | tsp. salt |
| ¼ | tsp. baking soda |
| ¼ | tsp. baking powder |

Heat milk to lukewarm and add yeast. Add sugar, shortening and egg. Mix dry ingredients and add to milk mixture. Knead on floured board.

Let rise, covered, until doubled. Punch down. Shape into 36 rolls. Let rise, covered, until doubled. Bake in 425° F oven for 15 minutes.

## YOGURT AND CHIVE ROLLS

¾  c. yogurt
2   tbsp. sugar
1   tsp. salt
2   tbsp. shortening
1   pkg. dry yeast
¼  c. warm water
2¼ c. flour
1   egg
1¼ tbsp. chopped chives

Mix yogurt, sugar, salt and shortening in saucepan. Bring to a boil and cool to lukewarm. Dissolve yeast in warm water in a mixing bowl and then stir in yogurt mixture and one half the flour. Beat until smooth. Add the rest of the flour, egg and chives and beat again. Scrape sides of bowl and cover with cloth. Let rise in a warm place until doubled. Grease 12 medium-sized muffin tins. Stir down batter and spoon until tins half full. Let rise until dough reaches the tops of the tins. Bake 15 minutes in a 400° F oven.

## BRAN / YOGURT MUFFINS

⅓  c. butter
½  c. sugar
1   large egg
1   c. yogurt
½  c. raisins
1   tbsp. molasses
1¼ c. bran
Dash of salt
1   tsp. nutmeg
1   tsp. baking soda
2   c. flour
½  c. walnuts, chopped

Cream butter; add sugar and egg. Beat well. Add yogurt, raisins, molasses and bran. Sift together salt, nutmeg, soda and flour; mix. Add nuts; mix again. Fill well-greased muffin tins ⅔ full. Bake 20 minutes at 375° F.

# YOGURT BISCUITS

¼    c. shortening
2    c. sifted flour
¼    tsp. baking soda
2¼    tsp. baking powder
1    tsp. salt
¾    c. thin yogurt

Preheat oven to 475° F. Cut shortening into flour until it has the texture of coarse cornmeal. Add baking soda to yogurt and stir into flour. Turn out on lightly floured board and cut with a floured cutter. Place on baking sheet for 10 to 12 minutes.

# WHOLE EARTH WHEAT GERM MUFFINS

½    c. vacuum packed wheat germ (regular)
1    c. stone ground whole wheat flour
½    c. all purpose flour
½    tsp. salt
1½    tsp. baking soda
½    c. sugar
½    c. seedless raisins
1    (8-oz.) carton plain yogurt
2    eggs
¼    c. vegetable oil

Combine wheat germ, flours, salt, soda, sugar and raisins. Mix yogurt, eggs and oil and pour over dry ingredients. Stir quickly and lightly to moisten dry ingredients. Do not beat. Spoon into 15 greased or paper lined 2½-inch muffin cups filling ¾ full. Bake in 400° F oven 18 to 20 minutes or until done. Serve warm with butter. Makes 15 muffins.

# YOGURT / CRANBERRY BISCUITS

2 c. flour
3 tsp. baking powder
¼ tsp. baking soda
1 tsp. salt
3 tbsp. shortening
1 egg
1 c. jellied cranberry sauce, crushed
¼ c. yogurt
**Grated cheese**

Sift dry ingredients together and cut in shortening. Beat egg and add cranberry sauce and yogurt. Add to dry ingredients and mix. Roll on a floured board and cut into squares. Place on baking sheet, sprinkle with grated cheese and bake 20 minutes in 400° F oven.

# YOGURT COFFEE CAKE

1½ c. sugar
½ lb. butter
2 eggs, beaten
1 c. yogurt
**Vanilla**
2 c. flour
1 tsp. baking powder
1 tsp. soda
**Dash of salt**
**Dash of cinnamon**
½ c. walnuts

Cream 1 c. sugar and butter. Add eggs. Add yogurt and vanilla to dry ingredients and add to the creamed mixture. Combine remaining sugar and nuts. Put half of the batter in a well-greased tube pan; pour in half of sugar-nut mixture. Add the remaining batter and nuts. Bake at 375° F for 45 minutes.

# CROWN JEWEL YOGURT CAKE

¾    c. (1½ sticks) butter
1    c. sugar
2    eggs
1    tsp. vanilla
1    ripe banana, peeled and mashed
2½   c. flour, sifted
1    tsp. baking soda
½    tsp. baking powder
½    tsp. salt
1    c. (8-oz. carton) plain yogurt
Currant Glaze (recipe follows)
1    banana, peeled and thinly sliced
Juice of one lemon
6    to 8 strawberries, hulled and sliced
½    c. California Thompson seedless grapes

Grease and dust with flour an 8- or 9-inch springform pan that is at least 2½ inches deep. Cream butter with sugar until light and fluffy. Add eggs, one at a time, beating after each addition. Add vanilla and banana. Sift together dry ingredients; combine one third of flour mixture with creamed mixture. Mix in *half* the yogurt. Alternate flour and yogurt until combined with creamed mixture. Pour batter into cake pan; bake in 350° F oven 1 hour and 15 minutes or until cake tests done. Let rest in pan a few minutes before turning out on cake rack to cool.

TO ASSEMBLE CAKE:  Place a piece of waxed paper under cake rack. Glaze cake liberally with Currant Glaze, reserving a couple of tablespoonsful. Arrange banana slices (dipped in lemon juice to prevent darkening) around rim of cake, the strawberries and grapes in center. Spoon reserved glaze over grapes. Garnish with additional grape clusters, if desired. Makes 8 to 10 servings.

CURRANT GLAZE
1    jar (10 oz.) currant jelly
1    tsp. grated orange rind
1    tsp. grated lemon rind

Combine currant jelly and rinds in a small saucepan and melt jelly over low heat.

# YOGURT CHOCOLATE CAKE

1½   sticks butter
1    lb. box light brown sugar
3    eggs
3    squares melted baking chocolate
2    tsp. vanilla
2¼   c. sifted cake flour
2    tsp. baking soda
¾    tsp. salt
½    c. thin yogurt
1    c. boiling water

Cream butter, brown sugar and eggs until light and fluffy. Add melted chocolate and vanilla. Sift together flour, salt and soda and add alternately with yogurt. Stir in boiling water. Pour in 9 x 13 inch pan. Bake at 350° F for 40 minutes.


# BANANA CAKE

2½   c. sifted cake flour
1⅔   c. sugar
1¼   tsp. baking powder
1    tsp. baking soda
1    tsp. salt
⅔    c. butter
1¼   c. mashed banana
⅔    c. yogurt
1    tsp. vanilla

Sift together flour, sugar, baking powder, soda and salt. Add butter, bananas and ⅓ c. yogurt. Stir slightly. Beat with electric mixer for 2 minutes. Add remaining yogurt, eggs and vanilla. Beat 2 minutes. Pour into 2 cake pans. Bake 35 minutes in 350° F oven.

# CHERRY CAKE

¾   c. soft butter
1½  c. sugar
3    eggs
1    tsp. baking soda
½   c. yogurt
½   tsp. allspice
½   tsp. cloves
1    c. cherries
2    c. sifted flour

Cream butter and sugar. Add eggs and beat well. Add soda to yogurt and stir into creamed mixture. Add spices and cherries, then flour. Mix well. Pour into 13 x 9 inch pan. Bake for 40 minutes at 350° F.

# DATE-ORANGE CAKE

1    c. shortening
2    c. sugar
4    eggs
1½  c. yogurt
1    tsp. baking soda
1    tsp. salt
4    c. cake flour
1    c. chopped dates
1    tsp. grated orange rind

Cream shortening, sugar and eggs. Add the rest of the ingredients and mix well. Put in a large greased tube pan. Bake at 350° F for 1 hour and 30 minutes.

SAUCE
2    c. sugar
1    c. orange juice
Grated rind of 1 orange

Combine and bring to boil. Pour hot sauce over hot cake. Let set until cold.

# YOGURT / PEACH PRESERVE CAKE

¾   c. butter
1    c. sugar
3    eggs, separated
2    c. sifted flour
⅛   tsp. salt
1    tsp. baking soda
½   c. thin yogurt
1    c. peach preserves

Cream butter and sugar. Stir in well-beaten yolks. Sift flour and measure. Add salt to flour. Stir soda into yogurt. Add flour mixture alternately with yogurt to the creamed mixture. Begin and end with flour. Lightly fold in peach preserves. Fold in stiffly beaten egg whites. Turn into 9-inch round layer cake pans. Bake in 350° F oven for 30 minutes. Cool on rack.

ICING
2    c. sugar
1    c. milk
1    c. coconut
1    c. crushed pineapple, drained
1    orange, ground and drained
1    c. chopped nuts

Cook sugar and milk to hard ball stage. Stir in coconut, pineapple, orange and nuts.

# CHOCOLATE WALNUT COOKIES

½   c. butter
1    c. sugar
1    egg
2    oz. melted chocolate
¾   c. thin yogurt
1    tsp. vanilla
1¾  c. flour
½   tsp. baking soda
½   tsp. salt
1    c. chopped walnuts

Preheat oven to 400° F. Mix shortening, sugar, egg and chocolate. Stir in yogurt and vanilla. Blend flour, salt and soda and add to other mixture. Mix in nuts and chill for an hour or more. Drop on lightly greased cookie sheet 2 inches apart. Bake 10 minutes.

## ORANGE / YOGURT COOKIES

2½  c. sugar
1    c. vegetable shortening
2    eggs
2    tsp. baking soda
1    c. thin yogurt
4½  c. flour
Juice and grated rind of 4 oranges
1    pkg. of confectioners' sugar
¼   c. butter, melted

Cream sugar and shortening; add eggs and beat well. Dissolve soda in yogurt. Add flour and yogurt alternately to sugar mixture and mix until light. Add half the juice and rind and mix. Drop on cookie sheet from teaspoon and bake at 350° F for 15 minutes. Cool and frost with mixture of confectioners' sugar, butter and remaining rind and juice.

## GINGER MOLASSES / YOGURT COOKIES

1    c. butter or margarine
1    c. sugar
2    eggs
1    c. molasses plus 1 tsp. baking soda
4    c. flour
2    tsp. ginger
1    tsp. cinnamon
½   tsp. salt
1    c. thin yogurt plus 1 tsp. baking soda

Cream butter and sugar until light; add eggs and molasses/soda. Sift dry ingredients together; add alternately with yogurt/soda. Drop by teaspoonful on greased baking sheet. Bake at 375° F for 12 minutes.

# MONTEREY PINEAPPLE CHEESECAKE

16    graham crackers, crushed
1    c. drained crushed pineapple
1½    lb. cream cheese
1    c. sugar
4    eggs
1    tsp. vanilla
2    c. yogurt

Put crumbs in bottom of large tube pan. Top with crushed pineapple. teaspoonful on greased baking sheet. Bake at 375° F for 12 minutes. for 1 hour.

# CREAM CHEESE AND YOGURT PIE

1½    c. vanilla wafers, crushed
½    c. melted butter
2    eggs
½    lb. cream cheese
1½    tsp. vanilla
½    c. plus 2 tbsp. sugar
1    c. yogurt

Combine crushed cookies and butter and line a pie plate with mixture. Chill. Beat eggs, cream cheese, 1 tsp. vanilla and ½ c. sugar and pour into chilled crust. Bake at 375° F for 20 minutes. Cool. Beat yogurt, 2 tbsp. of sugar and ½ tsp. vanilla. Pour on top of cooled pie. Then bake again at 475° F for 5 minutes. When cool chill again until ready to serve.

# YOGURT LEMON PIE

1    pkg. (4-serving size) lemon pudding and pie filling
1    c. sugar
¼    c. water
3    egg yolks
2    c. water
1    c. (½ pt.) plain yogurt
1    baked 10-inch pie shell, cooled
*3    egg whites
*6    tbsp. sugar

Combine pie filling mix, 1 c. sugar and ¼ c. water in a saucepan. Blend in egg yolks. Stir in 2 c. water and the yogurt, blending well. Cook and stir over medium heat until mixture comes to a *full bubbling boil.* Cool 5 minutes, stirring twice. Pour into pie shell.

Beat egg whites until foamy throughout. Gradually beat in 6 tbsp. sugar and continue beating until mixture will form stiff shiny peaks. Spread over pie filling, sealing edges well. Bake at 425° F about 5 minutes or until lightly browned. Cool 4 hours before cutting.

*For a higher meringue use 4 egg whites and ½ c. sugar.

## MONTEREY PIE

1½  c. cottage cheese
1    c. yogurt
1½  tbsp. honey
1    tsp. almond extract
1    banana

Mix together all the ingredients and fill a graham cracker pie shell with sliced banana, then yogurt mixture. Chill for several hours, then serve.

## FROZEN PEACH PIE

CRUST
1½  c. graham cracker crumbs
⅓   c. brown sugar, packed
½   tsp. cinnamon
⅓   c. melted butter or margarine
FILLING
1    can (29 oz.) cling peach slices
½   c. sugar
1    envelope (1 tbsp.) unflavored gelatin
2    eggs. separated
2    cartons (8 oz. each) plain yogurt
¼   tsp. almond extract
⅓   c. toasted coconut

**Crust:** Prepare crumbs in blender or place crackers in strong paper bag and roll fine with rolling pin. Place measured crumbs in medium bowl. Combine with remaining ingredients, tossing until well mixed.

With back of spoon press mixture to bottom and side of 9-inch pie plate, making small rim. Place in freezer until ready for filling.

**Filling:** Drain peaches, saving ½ c. syrup and ½ c. peach slices. Place all but ½ c. peaches into blender. Set aside. Blend ¼ c. sugar and gelatin in small saucepan. Stir peach liquid into mixture. Heat to a quick boil, stirring constantly. Blend into beaten yolks and quickly cover with plastic film. Cool. Blend in yogurt and peach puree. Beat egg whites at highest speed. Gradually beat in remaining sugar. Fold meringue into yogurt mixture, stirring in almond extract. Turn into frozen crumb pie crust. Freeze until firm (approximately 5 hours). Garnish with toasted coconut and remaining peach slices. Serves 6 to 8.

# FRESH GRAPE YOGURT PIE

| | |
|---|---|
| 2 | c. blue and green California grapes |
| 1 | c. "crunchy, whole-grain" breakfast cereal |
| 1 | envelope unflavored gelatin |
| ½ | c. cold water |
| 2 | egg yolks |
| 1 | tbsp. lemon juice |
| 1 | tsp. grated lemon rind *(optional)* |
| ⅓ | c. sugar |
| 1 | pkg. (8 oz.) cream cheese, softened |
| 1 | carton (8 oz.) plain or lime flavored yogurt |
| 4 | ice cubes |

Halve and seed grapes. Set aside. Prepare either crust as directed. Pat cereal into bottom and sides of buttered 9-inch pie plate; set aside. Sprinkle gelatin over cold water in small saucepan; heat over low heat until dissolved; set aside. Put egg yolks, lemon juice and rind, sugar, cream cheese and yogurt in blender; blend until smooth. Pour in dissolved gelatin; blend 5 seconds more. Add ice cubes, one at a time, blending smooth. Pour into prepared pie plate. Chill until mixture begins to set (about 10 minutes). Arrange grapes in concentric circles over surface. Chill until serving time. Makes 8 servings.

### GRAHAM CRACKER CRUST

Substitute 1¼ c. graham cracker crumbs for 1 c. crunchy breakfast cereal. Proceed as above.

# Yogurt Beverages

## BEVERAGES

One of our favorite ways of using yogurt is to drink it. The Armenians have a beverage which is served ice cold with meals on hot summer days. It's called Tan.

1½  c. creamy yogurt
1    qt. cold water
1    tbsp. honey
½    tsp. salt
Ice cubes

Mix together and serve with meals.

Gerry and I have had our most pleasurable yogurt experiences with "smoothies," yogurt drinks prepared in a blender. The most important thing to remember is anything goes. Experiment. Here are a few basic recipes.

## THE SMOOTHY

½    c. buttermilk
1½  c. milk
1    c. fruit juice, any kind
1    c. yogurt

You can add fresh fruit to make this even more tantalizing. Sliced cling peaches, for instance, or strawberries. Or combinations of these and others.

Sliced bananas
One egg
Pears
Mango
Papaya
Chocolate
Ovaltine
Orange juice
Tangerine juice
Crangrape, Cranorange, Cranapple or Cranberry
Frozen fruit (undefrosted)
Pineapple

If you like your smoothies more sweet than sour, add honey, jelly, molasses or juice from canned fruits for sweetener. Also, we use buttermilk as a creamy, complementary base, but you can do without it. This basic recipe of ours can be changed to suit your preferences, and it is *not* meant to be a standard, only a reference. The more juice you add the fruitier the smoothy and the more yogurt, the thicker and more tangy the drink will become. Add extra milk for more of a milk shake effect. Ice cubes added will make a delicious frosty-tasting smoothy. One healthful hint: don't throw away the whey, so to speak. This is the whitish liquid which sits on top of your yogurt, and it's loaded with vitamins. (you can drink whey all by itself with a little milk added.)

## BANANA 'N' ORANGE WHEAT GERM SHAKE

| | |
|---|---|
| 1 | small banana* |
| ¾ | cup milk or plain yogurt |
| ¼ | c. vacuum packed regular wheat germ |
| ¼ | c. orange juice |
| 1 | tbsp. honey |
| 1 | tsp. lemon juice |
| ⅛ | tsp. salt |
| 1 | ice cube |

*or medium fresh pear, peeled and cored

Slice banana into electric blender. Add remaining ingredients. Cover and blend at high speed about 30 seconds. Makes 1 (12-oz.) serving.

## PEACH WHEAT GERM SHAKE

1    medium fresh peach, peeled and pitted
1    (8-oz.) carton plain yogurt
¼    c. vacuum packed regular wheat germ
2    to 4 tbsp. brown sugar (packed)
⅛    tsp. cinnamon
1    ice cube

Combine all ingredients in electric blender. Cover and blend at high speed about 30 seconds. Makes 1 serving (1⅔ c.).

# *Yogurt Desserts & Snacks*

Making yogurt desserts and snacks is fun, easy and economical. Just take any preserves around the house—rasperries, peaches, or what you will—and mix them with plain yogurt or vanilla flavored yogurt. These will be equally delicious over fresh fruit, to which you may add a little sweetening.

## PEARS ELEGANT

Canned pears can grow a little tiresome after a while. Here's a way to add new zest: Mix the syrup from a can of pears with plain yogurt and use it as a topping for the fruit.

## SWEET AND SPECIAL

Try spooning honey or pancake syrup into plain yogurt or vanilla yogurt.

## APPLE SAUCE RAVE

Try mixing equal amounts of plain yogurt or vanilla flavored yogurt with apple sauce. Vary this combination by adding raisins or chopped walnuts and sprinkling with shredded coconut.

# FRUIT MOLD

Dissolve a package of raspberry flavored gelatin in water according to the instructions of the package. Chill until slightly thickened. Then blend it into a cup of vanilla flavored yogurt you have previously stirred. Fruit chunks may be added. Pour the mixture into individual small molds, or into a large one. For the sake of variety, try pouring into a 9 inch baked pie shell.

# YOGURT PEAR DELIGHT

| | |
|---|---|
| 1 | c. sugar |
| ¼ | c. lemon juice |
| 2 | tbsp. butter |
| 2 | c. boiling water |
| 8 | ripe pears |
| 2 | boxes frozen raspberries, thawed |
| ¼ | c. port wine |
| Yogurt | |

Simmer sugar, lemon juice, butter and water for 5 minutes. Peel pears and leave on stems. Arrange in a 3-qt. casserole dish. Add lemon mixture. Bake, covered, at 350° F for 45 minutes. Cool in liquid and drain. Mash raspberries and stir in wine. Lay pears in mixture and refrigerate overnight, turning occasionally and basting. Spoon yogurt over the top before serving.

# STRAWBERRIES WITH YOGURT

| | |
|---|---|
| 2 | pt. fresh strawberries, halved |
| ¼ | c. honey |
| 2 | c. yogurt |
| ¾ | tsp. vanilla |
| Mint | |

Mix strawberries and honey and chill. Mix yogurt and vanilla. Put strawberries in serving dish, top with yogurt and sprinkle with mint.

# CHERRIES AND YOGURT

| 2 | 1-lb. cans water packed cherries, well drained |
| 1 | 13½-oz. can pineapple chunks, drained |
| 1 | 3½-oz. coconut |
| ¾ | c. confectioners' sugar |
| ½ | tsp. salt |
| 2 | c. yogurt |
| Salad greens | |

Combine fruits, coconut, sugar and salt. Fold yogurt into mixture. Cover and refrigerate overnight. Garnish with salad greens.

# STRAWBERRY-BANANA

| 2 | pkg. strawberry gelatin |
| 1 | c. boiling water |
| 2 | 10-oz. pkg. frozen strawberries, thawed |
| 1 | 1-lb. 4-oz. can crushed pineapple, drained |
| 3 | medium bananas, mashed |
| 1 | c. chopped walnuts |
| 2 | c. yogurt |

Dissolve gelatin in boiling water, add all ingredients except yogurt. Mix well and pour half of the mixture into a 12 x 8 x 2 baking dish. Chill until firm. Spread yogurt over mixture, add remaining gelatin and chill until firm. 12 servings.

# BROILED GRAPE DELIGHT

| 2 | c. seedless grapes |
| 2 | c. yogurt |
| ¼ | c. honey |

Wash and stem grapes. Place in shallow baking dish. Spread yogurt over the grapes and drizzle honey on yogurt. Place under a broiler until yogurt is bubbly. 4 servings.

# APPLE-BUTTERED RUM PUDDING

2   c. half and half (cream and milk)
1   c. cooked rice
⅓   c. sugar
½   tsp. salt
1   envelope (1 tbsp) unflavored gelatin
¼   c. water
2   tbsp. rum
1   carton (8 oz.) yogurt (1 c.)
Apple Topping (follows)

Combine half and half, rice, sugar, and salt. Bring to a boil; reduce heat and simmer 20 mintues, stirring occasionally. Soften gelatin in water. Add to rice mixture and stir until gelatin dissolves. Cool until thickened but not set. Fold in rum and yogurt. Spoon into lightly oiled individual molds. Chill until firm. Unmold and serve with hot Apple Topping. Makes 6 servings (3 cups pudding).

### APPLE TOPPING

1½  to ¾ c. brown sugar
2   tsp. cornstarch
¼   tsp. salt
½   tsp. cinnamon
½   c. water
1   can (20 oz.) pie-sliced apples
1   tbsp. butter or margarine
2   tbsp. rum

Blend sugar, cornstarch, salt, cinnamon, and water. Add apples. Bring to a boil, reduce heat, and simmer 15 to 20 minutes or until apples are tender, stirring occasionally. Remove from heat. Add butter and rum. Serve hot over cold pudding (2⅓ c. topping.)

# SMOOTH PEACH AND ALMOND DESSERT

1⅓  c. light brown sugar
1   c. yogurt
1   tsp. almond extract
1   c. heavy cream
3¾  c. sliced fresh or well-drained canned peaches

Mix sugar, yogurt and almond extract until sugar is dissolved. Whip heavy cream until stiff and fold into yogurt mixture. Chill. Fold in peaches before serving.

## PEACH SHERBET

½   envelope unflavored gelatin
2   tbsp. cold water
2   c. thin yogurt
1   c. sugar
1   9-oz. can cling peaches, crushed
1   tsp. vanilla
1   egg white

Soften gelatin in cold water; dissolve over hot water. Combine yogurt, ¾ c. sugar, peaches, vanilla and gelatin; mix well. Pour in refrigerator tray. Freeze. Break in chunks and beat smooth. Beat egg white until peaks form and gradually add ¼ c. sugar beating to stiff peaks. Fold into peach mixture. Return to refrigerator tray and freeze until firm.

## PINEAPPLE YOGURT SHERBET

1   (8¼ oz.) can crushed pineapple
1½  tsp. unflavored gelatin
¾   c. sugar
⅛   tsp. salt
1   (16 oz.) container plain yogurt
1   tsp. lemon juice
1   tsp. grated lemon peel
½   tsp. vanilla
1   egg white

Turn pineapple into small saucepan, and sprinkle with gelatin. Let stand 5 minutes. Place over low heat, and stir until gelatin dissolves. Remove from heat. Set aside 2 tbsp. sugar for egg white. Stir remaining sugar and salt into pineapple. Cool to room temperature. Stir in yogurt, lemon juice and peel, and vanilla. Turn into loaf pan, about 1½ quarts capacity. Freeze until firm. When mixture is frozen, beat egg white to soft peaks. Beat in reserved 2 tbsp. sugar, a little at a time, making a meringue. Turn sherbet into large chilled bowl, and beat at low speed until smooth. Increase speed and beat until fluffy. Fold in meringue. Return sherbet to pan and freeze firm. Makes a generous quart.

## LOW CALORIE PINK LADY PARFAIT

2    cartons (8 oz. *each*) plain yogurt
2    to 4 tbsp. sugar
1    pkg. (10 oz.) frozen sliced strawberries in syrup, partially thawed
2    egg whites
Garnish: whipped cream and whole frozen strawberries (optional)

In blender, whirl yogurt, sugar, ¼ c. of the berries, egg whites and ice cubes. Pour into shallow pan and freeze until almost firm. Place in mixing bowl. Beat at high speed until smooth. Refreeze until almost firm. Meanwhile, pour remaining berries into saucepan. Mix 1½ tbsp. sugar and 1 tsp. cornstarch. Stir into berries. Bring to boil. Cook and stir 2 minutes, or until sauce is slightly thick. Remove from heat. Add 1½ tsp. lemon juice. Chill. Spoon alternate layers of yogurt ice and strawberry sauce into 4 parfait glasses, beginning with ice and ending with sauce. Refreeze. Fifteen minutes before serving time, remove from freezer to thaw slightly. Garnish with whipped cream and a whole frozen strawberry, if desired. Serve at once. Makes 4 servings.

## CRANBERRY PEACH MOUSSE

1    pkg. (3 oz.) lemon gelatin
1    can (29 oz.) sliced cling peaches, drained
2    pkg. (3 oz. each) strawberry gelatin
2    c. boiling cranberry juice
1    c. cranberry-orange relish
2    c. plain yogurt
Whipped cream or topping

Prepare lemon gelatin according to package directions using only 1½ c. water. Chill gelatin until syrupy. Arrange 6 to 8 of the peach slices in a pretty pattern on the bottom of 1½ quart mold. Dice remaining peaches. Spoon gelatin carefully into mold keeping pattern intact. Chill until almost firm. Meanwhile, dissolve strawberry gelatin in cranberry juice. Beat in relish and yogurt. Chill until slightly thickened.

Fold diced peaches into cranberry gelatin mixture. Spoon this mixture over lemon gelatin and chill until firm. To unmold dip mold into lukewarm water for a few seconds. Tap to loosen and invert onto a platter. Spoon whipped cream or topping around mold and serve at once. Makes one 1½ quart mold.

## BOYSENBERRY MOUSSE

| | |
|---|---|
| 2 | envelopes unflavored gelatin |
| ½ | c. sugar, divided |
| ⅛ | tsp. salt |
| 3 | eggs, separated |
| 1 | c. milk |
| 2 | c. all-natural lowfat yogurt, boysenberry |
| 1 | c. heavy cream |

Combine gelatin, ¼ c. sugar and salt in medium saucepan. Mix together yolks and milk in medium bowl and stir into gelatin. Place over low heat; stir constantly until gelatin dissolves, about 5 minutes. Cool slightly and add yogurt. Chill, stirring occasionally, until mixture mounds slightly when dropped from a spoon. Beat egg whites until soft peaks form, beat in remaining ¼ c. sugar and beat until stiff. Whip heavy cream until stiff. Fold egg whites and whipped cream into boysenberry mixture. Turn into 8-cup mold and chill several hours or overnight. 10 servings.

## WESTERN DESSERT SALAD

| | |
|---|---|
| 1 | small head western iceberg lettuce |
| Dessert Salad Dressing (follows) | |
| 1 | large banana |
| 1 | medium-size orange |
| 1 | medium-size pink grapefruit |
| ½ | c. sliced strawberries |

Core, rinse and thoroughly drain lettuce; refrigerate in disposable plastic bag or plastic crisper. Shortly before serving, prepare Dessert Salad Dressing, using half the banana. Pare and section orange and grapefruit; slice remaining half banana. Combine with strawberries. Shred lettuce to measure 1 quart. Place ½ c. lettuce in bottom of each of 4 serving bowls. Spoon ¼ c. fruit over each, and top with 2 tbsp. dressing. Repeat layers. Makes 4 servings.

### DESSERT SALAD DRESSING

In blender jar, combine ¼ c. yogurt, 1 medium-size orange, pared and sectioned, ½ banana, 1 tbsp. each honey and lemon juice, 1 tsp. grated orange peel and ¼ tsp. salt. Cover and blend smooth. Makes 1 c. dressing.

# OLD GLORY BLOX

| | |
|---|---|
| 6 | envelopes unflavored gelatin |
| 10 | tbsp. sugar |
| 3½ | c. boiling water |
| 1 | can (15 oz.) blueberries in light syrup, undrained |
| 1 | c. (8 oz.) plain yogurt |
| 1 | pkg. (10 oz.) frozen raspberries in syrup, thawed |

### BLUE LAYER

In large bowl, mix 2 envelopes unflavored gelatin and 4 tbsp. sugar. Add 1 c. boiling water and stir until gelatin is completely dissolved; stir in blueberries. Pour into 9'' x 13'' shallow baking pan and chill until almost set. Meanwhile prepare white layer.

### WHITE LAYER

In large bowl, mix 2 envelopes unflavored gelatin and 2 tbsp. sugar. Add 1 c. boiling water and stir until gelatin is completely dissolved. With wire whip or rotary beater, blend in yogurt. Carefully pour onto Blue Layer and chill until almost set. Meanwhile, prepare Red Layer.

### RED LAYER

In large bowl, mix 2 envelopes unflavored gelatin and 4 tbsp. sugar. Add 1½ c. boiling water and stir until gelatin is completely dissolved; stir in raspberries. Carefully pour onto White Layer and chill until firm. Cut into squares and serve. Makes about 10 dozen (1-inch) squares.

# BACK TO NATURE BLOX

4 envelopes unflavored gelatin
½ c. cold water
1 c. boiling water
¼ c. honey
2 containers (8 oz. ea.) fruit-flavored yogurt

In large bowl, sprinkle unflavored gelatin over cold water. Add boiling water and stir until gelatin is completely dissolved; stir in honey. With wire whisk or rotary beater, blend in yogurt. Pour into 8- or 9-inch square pan and chill until firm. Cut into squares to serve. Makes about 5 to 6 dozen squares.

# A (Head To-) Footnote:
# Yogurt Cosmetics

Lately, people talk a lot about the magical properties of herbs and plants. Mutton lotion, distilled water, beef marrow, mud, hog's lard, buttermilk, goose fat, rose water, barley glop and yogurt are among the many popular natural cures for clogged pores, sluggish bowels, headaches, dry scalp, brittle hair, and other maladies of the head and heart, both imagined and real.

Parisian beauty expert, Madeleine Plaz, is said to use two soup-spoons of plain yogurt in each herbal shampoo which she gives. The casein content, she explained, sheathed the hair in a thin coating for protection against wind and pollution. In a barrage of freshly tuned interest, major women's magazines have recommended yogurt as a douche, for breast massage and daily bath.

Yogurt is an excellent source of calcium, phosphorous, and many of the B vitamins necessary for the health of your skin. This may be why one of the fastest-growing cosmetic uses of yogurt is as a douche. In the presence of yeast infections, it has been reported that yogurt has, in a number of cases, brought about a cure. Some doctors advise women to use yogurt when they are treating infections with antibiotics, since these drugs are known to kill the healthy bacteria in the vaginal tract.

Anne Carpenter, who founded her own cosmetics company (see directory listing) at the age of twenty-seven, and who now at the age of thirty is a widely-known authority on natural cosmetics for health and beauty, has written the following: "Being a live food, yogurt offers much for the home cosmetic chemist. The beneficial bacteria found in this marvelous food is not only good for the system when taken internally, but is an excellent base or additive when used to condition the skin. Yogurt is a source of high quality protein, which because of its natural acidity, is compatible with the skin's acid mantle.''

The following cosmetic recipes are gratefully printed here through the cooperation of Anne Carpenter.

## YOGURT OATMEAL MASQUE

½   **c. quick cooking oats**
**Water**
¼   **c. yogurt**

Cook oatmeal with water for a minute or so. Make the paste a little thicker than normally made for eating. Add the yogurt and blend well. Mashed banana may be added for extra beneficial qualities. Apply to the face and relax for 15 minutes to ½ hour. Rinse with warm water. Your skin will feel silky smooth. Oatmeal offers the skin protein and a milky substance which helps to soothe irritated skin.

Yogurt also makes a marvelous balm for sunburn. Mixing with apricots makes an even more beneficial healer for sunburn. After exposure to wind and weather a yogurt bath is delightful for a smoother you from head to toe.

## YOGURT BATH

1    **c. yogurt**
3    **tbsp. Epsom Salts**
2    **tbsp. Wheat Germ oil**
10   **Drops perfume oil**

Mix all ingredients together and add to your bath as the water is running. Sit back and enjoy what all those natural ingredients are doing for your skin.

Yogurt and heavy cream mixed together makes an excellent cuticle softener before manicuring. Mix yogurt and cream together in a small bowl and warm to room temperature. Soak fingertips in this mixture for about ten minutes. After soaking gently push back the excess cuticle with the blunt end of a wooden stick made for this purpose. Never cut or rip the excess skin.

Yogurt also makes an excellent skin cleanser, especially mixed with cornmeal or ground almonds. Mix whole or skimmed milk yogurt (depending if your skin is oily or dry) with almonds you have ground by hand, or in your blender, or cornmeal right from the package. Using a wash cloth or your fingertips, massage the blend onto the skin in a small circular pattern with your fingers. The massaging not only lifts off dead skin cells, but exercises the collagen fiber in the tissues of the skin. (Collagen is what keeps the skin tight and elastic.)

Plain whole-milk yogurt makes a great acidifier for hair which has been treated with permanents or colorings. These products are highly alkaline and strip the hair of its natural acidity. Massage yogurt into the hair and scalp. Let this sit on the hair for at least half an hour before shampooing. Shampoo the hair with a non-alkaline or mildly acid shampoo, and follow with a conditioner, which is also mildly acid. This acid treatment should bring back the luster to tired hair.

Yogurt can be included in many home face cream or moisturizer recipes. A simple lotion recipe calls for cucumbers and yogurt all whirled up in a blender. Cucumber not only softens the skin, but helps to evenly lighten a faded tan. The addition of lemon to this recipe would also be effective for lightening the skin. The following is a recipe for a body lotion that is just chock full of goodness for the skin. Use the cleanest utensils and remember to refrigerate any leftovers. Canning jars are perfect storage jars for any of your kitchen cosmetology recipes.

## BODY LOTION

1   tbsp. whipped margarine melted
2   tbsp. safflower oil
1   whole egg
¼   c. yogurt
6   tbsp. whole milk
2   tbsp. witch hazel
½   c. apple juice
Few drops vinegar

Place egg, oil and margarine in a blender or large mixing bowl, blend well, add other ingredients, mixing well after each addition. When all ingredients have been mixed use the mixture all over the body for an extra special body lotion.

Another simple recipe is:

## DRY SKIN MASQUE

¼   c. yogurt
½   avocado

Mix well together. Use on the face for 15 to 20 minutes and rinse with warm water.

A widely known beauty editor and co-author of *Beauty Is No Big Deal,* Donna Lawson has written a complete guide to hundreds of beauty preparations made from fruits, herbs, milk products, grains, honey and other wholesome, easy-to-find ingredients.

She writes: "There are many reasons, aside from ecological ones, to learn about homemade natural beauty preparations. For one, time has proved their effectiveness . . . our grandmothers, and their grandmothers made beauty preparations at home on the wood stove." She also states that "Sixty thousand Americans suffer allergic reactions to commercial cosmetics each year. Sometimes the effects are even more serious . . ."

In her book, *Mother Nature's Beauty Cupboard* (Thomas Y. Crowell 1973, Bantam 1974), she offers a number of beauty recipes which use yogurt, and the following are reprinted with thanks to her and her publishers.

## FOR THE SKIN

**YOGURT CLEANSER:**
Plain yogurt makes an excellent skin cleanser, applied either directly from the container or with herbs added. A capsule can be punctured and the contents mixed with yogurt. Wipe or rinse it off and follow with cold water.

**YOGURT-CREAM-ALMOND-SALT CLEANSER:**
Yogurt, cream, and crushed almonds in equal amounts and a pinch of sea salt placed in a muslin bag, then moistened and rubbed over the face, make a good cleaning agent for oily skin. Rinse first with warm water, then with cold. Follow with a freshener if you like.

**YOGURT, MINT AND FULLER'S EARTH MASK:**
For deep pore-cleaning action, beauty rest and skin nourishment mix

one teaspoon peppermint extract with one tablespoon water. Add enough yogurt and fuller's earth (available at drug stores) in equal parts to make a paste. Apply the mask to the skin and leave it on 10 to 15 minutes. Rinse it off with warm water, then a dash of cold. The mint gives the skin a menthol feeling.

### SWAMI HARIHARDAS' WRINKLE-REMOVER:
Carefully blend one teaspoon rice powder with one teaspoon each grapefruit juice, carrot juice, and yogurt. Keep in the sun for three hours. Apply to the face overnight to smooth out wrinkles.

### MARIGOLD MASSAGE OINTMENT:
Dried flowers and leaves from a marigold are made into a tea (with flowers strained out) and mixed with yogurt to make a massage cream for your feet. Marigolds are traditionally used to heal sprains, wounds, and varicose veins. Personally, I haven't seen them work in these three areas, but I know this ointment eases aches in my feet.

# FOR THE HAIR:

### EAST INDIAN PEANUT CONDITIONER:
In India women use this conditioner to restore oils that have been dried out by the sun. Use equal amounts peanut flour (can be found at health food stores), lemon juice and yogurt. Scrub the mixture into the hair and wash it out with Dr. Bronner's or with castile shampoo and warm water. Follow up with a vinegar rinse for a terrific protein conditioning. Note: If peanut flour can't be found, ask the proprietor of a health food store to grind up peanuts for you.

### YOGURT-LEMON RIND BLEACHED HAIR CONDITIONER:
Combine equal amounts yogurt and grated lemon rind (1 tsp. each for shorter hair, more for longer). Generously rub this into the scalp, pulling it through the hair. Yogurt, with its natural concentrated protein, nourishes dry, sun- or chemical-bleached hair; the lemon rind adds natural oils and luster.

### EGG YOLK-YOGURT CONDITIONER FOR DULL, BRITTLE HAIR:
Beat one egg yolk until fluffy. To it add ½ cup yogurt and beat until thoroughly mixed. Comb this mixture through clean hair. Leave it on for ten minutes, then rinse thoroughly with warm water. Follow up with a vinegar rinse and more warm water. This leaves the hair soft and lustrous.

# *Yogurt Natural Foods Directory*

The following list is given to acquaint readers with a few natural foods companies which deal in yogurt products. Many publish pamphlets and bulletins from time to time. And some also supply information on request.

ALTA-DENA DAIRY
637 Hambledon
City of Industry, California 91744

    Fresh milk, kefir, yogurt, ice cream,
    other dairy products.

ANNE CARPENTER'S COSMETICS
Route 100
Weston, Vermont 05161

CALIFORNIA GOAT DAIRYMEN'S ASSOCIATION
P.O. Box 934
Turlock, California 95380

    Miracle Evaporate Goat Milk
    Miracle Powdered Goat Milk

COLOMBO YOGURT, INC.
One Dantan Drive
Menthuen, Massachusetts 01844

## CONTINENTAL YOGURT COMPANY
1354 East Colorado Street
Glendale, California 91205

Freeze dried Kefir Grains, Acidophilus Culture,
Royal Yogurt—plain or with fruit preserves,
also low-fat Kefir Cheese and Kefir nonfat yogurt drink

## DANKA'S ORIGINALS
17100 Burton Street
Van Nuys, California 91406

Distributes Yogamatic yogurt makers, cottage cheese makers,
dry yogurt and cheese cultures and rennet.

## DANNON MILK PRODUCTS
23-11 38th Avenue
Long Island City, New York 11101

## ERIVAN YOGURT
1984 Audobon Drive
Dresher, Pennsylvania 19025

Erivan Yogurt, whole milk—acidophilus culture.

## THE GATES HOMESTEAD FARMS
Manlius-Chittenango Road
Chittenango, New York 13037

Unheated (Raw) certified milk, Rifek. (Rikef is kefir spelled
backwards due to N.Y. state regulations.)

## CHRIS HANSEN'S LABORATORY, INC.
9015 West Maple Street
Milwaukee, Wisconsin 53214

Hansen's Rennet Tablets, Yogurt and Acidophilus Cultures,
Yogurt Tablets.

INTERNATIONAL YOGURT COMPANY
628 North Doheny Drive
Los Angeles, California 90069

International Yogurt Face Cream Concentrate, Yogurt Face and
Body Powder, Yogurt Tablets, Kefir Grains, Kefir Culture,
Dry Original Bulgarian Yogurt Culture, Thermo-Cult Electirc
Yogurt Incubator, Yogomatic Yogurt Incubator, fresh cheese
culture, acidophilus culture.

SALTON, INC.
1260 Zarega Avenue
Bronx, New York 10462

Ice cream machine, Egg Cooker, Yogurt Maker.